SUPERHINTS
FOR LIFE

Also compiled by The Lady Wardington

❖❖❖ SUPERHINTS ❖❖❖
FOR LIFE

Personal, Practical and Perspicacious

Compiled by
The Lady Wardington

MICHAEL JOSEPH
LONDON

MICHAEL JOSEPH LTD

Published by the Penguin Group
27 Wrights Lane, London W8 5TZ
Viking Penguin Inc., 375 Hudson Street, New York,
New York 10014, USA
Penguin Books Australia Ltd, Ringwood, Victoria, Australia
Penguin Books Canada Ltd, 10 Alcorn Avenue, Toronto,
Ontario, Canada, M4V 3B2
Penguin Books (NZ) Ltd, 182–190 Wairau Road, Auckland 10,
New Zealand

Penguin Books Ltd, Registered Offices: Harmondsworth,
Middlesex, England

First published 1997

Typeset in Goudy 10/12½ point
Printed in England by Clays Ltd, St Ives plc

A CIP catalogue record for this book is available from the
British Library

ISBN 0 7181 4280 2

The hints in this book are intended to suggest possible
solutions only. While every effort has been made to check
their accuracy, the compiler, contributors and publisher
can neither guarantee absolute success nor accept any legal
responsibility or liability for their effectiveness.

❖❖❖ Contents ❖❖❖

This one is for Marion, too.

Oh, that she were here to
enjoy the hints with me.

FOREWORD

This is the fourth *Superhints* book I have compiled to raise money for the Katharine House Hospice near Banbury, Oxfordshire. The first book came out in November 1991 and by coincidence the Hospice opened at the same time.

In the last six years the palliative care it has been able to offer terminally ill people through the home-care nurses and the day-care centre is impossible to quantify. Since the opening of the Hospice, ten in-patient beds offering respite to carers as well as terminal care for patients have been added. The bereavement team strengthens the spirit of sufferers and their loved ones alike, and a vast number of volunteers bring any special skills they have to help – as diverse as aromatherapy, flower arranging, massage and t'ai chi – as well as taking patients on shopping expeditions, playing Scrabble or even bringing a PAT dog to be stroked.

All this care and special attention costs a fortune. At least half has to be raised by the Hospice itself, towards which these books help a bit. Their great advantage over other forms of fund-raising (because I hate having to ask people for money) is that I haven't had to badger my friends and acquaintances to buy tickets to balls, take tombola or raffle tickets, or even support marathon runners: in this instance it really is a case of 'it's the thought that counts'. And how marvellously all the contributors have risen to the challenge. People from every walk of life have cudgelled their brains to come up with diverse, caring and practical ideas which will, I hope, enrich the readers' lives. Without the generous spirit of all these wonderful well-wishers, the books could not possibly have got off the ground, and any success they have had has been due entirely to them. And I couldn't have completed the compilation without my dear friend Laurie Purden, former editor of *Woman's Journal,* who has held my hand and been an indefatigable hint-hunter from the very beginning.

I have not resisted the temptation to include a lot of my own hints and I particularly wanted to include my own special 'Superhint for life'. I felt, however, that it was too long to be in the body of the book so I am using my compiler's privilege to put it here. Well known as the 'Desiderata', it was found in a crevice in a church in Baltimore when it was being renovated in the 1950s. Although the original is dated 1692, it seems to me to embody all the essentials for the happiness of life today.

> Go placidly amid the noise and haste, and remember what peace there may be in silence. As far as possible without surrender, be on good terms with all persons. Speak your truth quietly and clearly, and listen to others, even the dull and ignorant: they too have their story. Avoid loud and aggressive persons: they are vexations to the spirit. If you compare yourself with others, you may become vain and bitter; for always there will be greater and lesser persons than yourself.
>
> Enjoy your achievements as well as your plans. Keep interested in your own career, however humble; it is a real possession in the changing fortunes of time. Exercise caution in your business affairs, for the world is full of trickery. But let this not blind you to what virtue there is: many persons strive for high ideals, and everywhere life is full of heroism.
>
> Be yourself. Especially, do not feign affection. Neither be cynical about love, for in the face of all

aridity and disenchantment it is as perennial as the grass.

Take kindly the counsel of years, gracefully surrendering the things of youth. Nurture strength of spirit to shield you in sudden misfortune. But do not distress yourself with imaginings. Many fears are born of fatigue and loneliness. Beyond a wholesome discipline, be gentle with yourself.

You are a child of the universe, no less than the trees and the stars; you have a right to be here. And whether or not it is clear to you, no doubt the universe is unfolding as it should. Therefore be at peace with God, whatever you conceive Him to be, and whatever your labours and aspirations, in the noisy confusion of life keep peace with your soul. With all its sham, drudgery and broken dreams, it is still a beautiful world. Be careful. Strive to be happy.

Many of the hints in this book echo the advice in this comforting piece. I hope you, the reader, will enjoy them and find them both useful and encouraging.

Audrey Wardington

ALL IN A DAY'S WORK

Money is like a sixth sense without which you cannot make complete use of the other five.

W. SOMERSET MAUGHAM

SPECIALIZE

The advice I would give to anyone starting out in the job market is to specialize in one particular area. Ideally, it helps to choose an occupation that hasn't been trawled by everybody else, but whatever you do, aim to make yourself indispensable and the best there is. That way, you will always be in demand.

Christie Hickman
Journalist

INCURABLE

Megalomania is the vocational disease of newspaper proprietors. The symptoms are egocentricity and the illusion of infallibility. There is no known cure.

The Lord Cudlipp

PAVE YOUR WAY

There is no such thing as a career path – it is crazy paving and you have to lay it yourself.

Dominic Cadbury
Chairman, Cadbury Schweppes

TAKE A TIP

If a director of a company advises you to buy its shares, expect to halve your money; if the chairman recommends the purchase you will lose the lot; but if you invest on a tip from a taxi-driver you will make a fortune.

Richard Good
Banker

GOOD BUSINESS

Make friends with those you do business with, but never do business with friends.

Norman Hudson
Publisher

SEEING IS BELIEVING

Believe ninety per cent of what you see and only ten per cent of what you hear.

The Lord Wolverton

ALL PASSION SPENT

A tip for those who have to deal with the public on the telephone. Just occasionally when fielding a complaint you will be confronted by someone who loses their temper. If you find yourself on the receiving end of an intemperate tirade, wait for it to run its course, then say apologetically, 'I am so sorry, there seems to be a fault on the line and I didn't catch a word you said. Would you mind repeating it?' Since few people can sustain the same level of spontaneous fury when forced to rerun it, the communication will be measured and restrained the second time round.

Philip Hook
Art expert and author

SPEAK CLEARLY, PLEASE

Answerphones are a boon and a blessing to anyone who works from home or is often out, but they can also be a source of some irritation if you don't know the caller and are so busy trying to decypher their message that you miss – or mishear – the return-call number and have to replay the tape to find out. Should you be the caller, make sure you give your name and number clearly (don't gabble) and, if necessary, repeat it after your message. The same principle applies to fax owners whose fax and phone numbers are the same. Here, the ideal message to leave is: 'This is (phone number). I'm not here to take your call, but leave your message and I'll get back to you. If you want to transmit a fax, the number is the same as the telephone which is (repeat phone number).' This not only saves time but is better for the blood pressure.

Colin McDowell
Fashion historian

GET AHEAD

Whenever you have a good idea, act on it quickly. If you don't, you can bet your life someone else will get in first.

Sir Cliff Richard
Singer and actor

FIND TIME

Many years ago I decided never again to use the excuse 'I don't have time.' For some reason this had a quite magical effect. Ever since then, I *have* had time. Things often get done late, but they do get done.

Chris Kelly
TV producer and presenter

BIT BY BIT

If any job seems dauntingly large, split it up into a lot of limited day tasks and give yourself strict deadlines. As a reward, however, allow yourself to knock off early once you have completed the day's assignment. This goes for getting the best out of others too.

Sir Antony Jay
Writer and producer

HOLIDAY TASK

When I was a student looking for a holiday job in Martha's Vineyard I answered all the 'jobs vacant' advertisements for the sort of task I could do – gardening, trash collection, window washing, etc. I was always fifteenth in line, and so I decided to approach the problem from a different angle. I looked for firms advertising the sort of service that my non-skills fitted and went to them direct, thus being first in the queue if they were even considering taking on extra staff. On my third go I got a job collecting trash and had a wonderful summer.

Eliot Pierce
Student at Brown University, USA

DO IT NOW

When you see something misplaced in the house, don't just say 'Oh, there it is, I'll put it in the right place later.' DO IT NOW. Later, you won't remember where it was you saw it. When something you ought to do swims into your mind, DO IT NOW. Later, you'll remember remembering but not what it was you remembered. If there's a difficult telephone call to be made, DO IT NOW. The impulse to do a kind act or send a grateful message can pass very quickly, so DO IT NOW.

Victoria Glendinning
Author and journalist

SOUND ADVICE

I remember Sir Alec Douglas-Home quoting some advice given to him by his father-in-law. 'When a man says his word is as good as his bond, always take his bond.'

Hugo Vickers
Biographer

DIMINISHING RETURN

The less the power, the greater the desire to exercise it.

Bernard Levin
Journalist and author

IGNORANCE IS NOT BLISS

If you think training is expensive, try ignorance. Without it you cannot compete or improve – you are dead.

Dominic Cadbury
Chairman, Cadbury Schweppes

BOUNCER

The first intimation you get that a bill isn't going to be paid is when the debtor tells you that the cheque is in the post.

Richard Good
Banker

NEVER A LENDER

Never lend money, only give it. If the sum is too large to lose without a care, it is too large to come between you and a friend.

The Lord Wardington

THE WAITING GAME

If somebody doesn't need an answer until Thursday, never give them the answer on Wednesday. Procrastination may be the thief of time but precipitation invariably leads to disaster.

Alan Titchmarsh
Gardening journalist and TV presenter

TIP FROM THE TOP

I followed this maxim when I left the *Today* programme and it applies to all sorts of activities, particularly in the sporting and entertainment world – 'quit while you're winning.'

John Timpson
Writer and broadcaster

SELL, SELL

If your house hasn't attracted a bid even after twenty-five people have looked at it, lower the price. The market's talking to you and you should

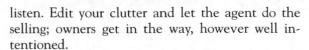

listen. Edit your clutter and let the agent do the selling; owners get in the way, however well intentioned.

Barbara Pierce
New York real estate agent

SELL BY SMELL

There are two things you can do that will help if you are trying to sell your house. When a prospective purchaser rings the doorbell, fill the house with the smell of proper coffee and baking bread. You don't need to go to all the fag of actually making the bread. Stockpile half-baked baguettes instead. And a coffee bean burnt on the hot-plate will fill the house with a proper coffee aroma.

Anna Pavord
Gardening writer, The Independent

DEBATABLE

I always go to the girl clerk at the Post Office, railway station, etc. – she will be three times quicker than a man.

Alan Tyser
Retired stockbroker

GOOD TIMING

Successful tycoons, it is said, always have their colds on Fridays. This is generally taken to mean that their subconscious minds know they must not interrupt their work. In fact it means that their subconscious minds are clever enough to get them out of cutting the grass and putting up shelves.

Katharine Whitehorn
Journalist

ON FORM

Intelligence is in inverse proportion to the ability to fill in forms correctly.

David Scott-Gatty
Financial adviser

STICK TO SCHEDULE

When writing the agenda for a meeting, put the starting time against each item; then people will realize that if they spend too long on one subject they're not going to get away on time.

Sir Antony Jay
Writer and producer

LIST IT

Faced with 101 things to do in a day with no idea where to start or which to do first, do what I do:

1. Make a cup of coffee and sit down.
2. Write on a piece of paper the numbers 1 to 10. Then prioritize the ten most important things that need doing.
3. Finish the coffee, then start to do the task at the top of the list. Do not stop until it is done.
4. Once it is finished, take a breather (toilet, phone calls, more coffee). Then undertake the second item on the list. Don't stop until you have finished that one.

Carry on like this until all ten have been completed. If, however, by the end of the day there are jobs left undone, the chances are they weren't that important anyway and so can be left until tomorrow. There will definitely be a feel-good factor in achieving a lot.

Graham Clarke
Editor, Amateur Gardening

GIFT OF THE GAB

Thoughts on public speaking:

Know your subject; marshal your thoughts; make careful, logical notes. Then leave your spectacles at home, and make a really spontaneous speech.

Barry Lane
Former Chief Executive, Cardiff Bay Development

MONEY TALKS

Conversing with automatic cash dispensers is perfectly understandable and not as uncommon as you might think.

Lynne Truss
Writer and novelist

AD-LIB

Accept after-dinner speaking engagements only if they are received with less than three hours' notice. You then have the perfect excuse if everything goes wrong – and the chances are it will be fine because you will not have had time to prepare anything complicated.

Jo Cornley
Director of Administration and Finance,
Katharine House Hospice

POLITESSE

In business, as in your personal life, there's no excuse for not answering letters. Even if you haven't time to reply immediately, a few words to say that the letter has arrived and you will be writing in full later will comfort the sender – and diffuse their impatience.

Susan Watt
Associate Publisher, Michael Joseph Ltd

DELEGATION

Spread the load – don't be a martyr and try to do everything yourself; get someone else to do it for you but make sure they are capable and enthusiastic. Delegation is the key to most things, as is careful forward planning.

Angela Perry
Fundraising consultant

MEMO TO BOSS

Printed notice to be framed and hung on the wall behind the manager's desk: 'Have *you* a solution or are *you* part of the problem?'

John Ewart
Industrialist

IN POCKET

Buy jewellery for love, never for investment. That way your heart may get broken but your pocket will remain intact.

Richard Sancroft-Baker
Jeweller

GO FOR IT

If you are a collector and you see something you really like, buy it, even if you think you can't afford it, and always keep the receipt.

Dr Alan Borg
Director General, Victoria & Albert Museum

WHAT AM I TO BID?

Buying at auction can be thrilling but it is easy to get carried away. If the lot you want is going to be pricey, get a dealer to bid for you. You will have to pay him commission, but other dealers may not bid against him as they would an outsider – and he will stick to your ceiling.

The Lord Wardington

AT EASE

Interviewing an applicant for a job can be as stressful for the interviewer as the interviewee, and if the latter is nervous it is particularly difficult to make proper assessment of their character. I have found that if I can start off by asking them to help me to do something – open a window which has stuck, lift a heavy box, move a piece of furniture even – the ice will be broken and we can sit down together more comfortably, even companionably, particularly if they have been made to feel strong and useful.

The Hon. Mrs Pease

NO BYPASS

Never try to bypass the great man's secretary – get her on your side.

Katharine Whitehorn
Journalist

SPIKE THOSE BILLS

The worst part of running your own business if you're a one-man band is doing the accounts for the accountant (a bit like cleaning up for the cleaning lady). When the VAT is due, or the tax man summoneth, sorting through a boxful of receipts is tedious and time-consuming. A spike cuts the work in half. From the start, spike your receipts on it day by day. Then, at the end of each quarter or year, it's all on the spike in date order.

Anne Gregg
Journalist and broadcaster

DIARY OF EVENTS

If you are going through any experience (noisy neighbours, serious disagreements with business partners, a difficult divorce that you think might eventually lead to litigation), keep a meticulous 'diary of events'. A record of each occurrence, written down at the time it actually happens, is much more valuable than generalizations and could well be accepted as evidence in court.

John Moss
Retired solicitor

PROMISES

Never threaten to do something unless you are prepared, if events so turn out, to implement the threat. If you are not so prepared the expressed threat could rebound on you.

The Lord Aberconway

A WRITE-OFF

Never write anything in anger or passion that you wouldn't want to hear repeated in a court of law or read in a newspaper.

The Lady Cudlipp

THINK IT THROUGH

In your actions, as with your temper, try not to be precipitate. Instead, when you have a chance, think out the consequences of each alternative action and choose the one with the best (least worst) likely results.

Sir Richard Lloyd
Former Chairman, Vickers

KEEPING IN TOUCH

*To err is human but to really foul things up
needs a computer.*

ANON.

READY TO RUB

Keep your diary in pencil so that you can keep it
up-to-date and make changes. Use a slim handbag-
sized book rather than having to depend on a bulky
Filofax.

Lady Celestria Noel
Social Editor, Harpers & Queen

ROOM FOR MANOEUVRES

'What on earth are you doing?' asked my wonderfully
organized, cross-indexed famous friend, Shirley
Conran. What I was doing was scribbling yet another
change of phone/fax/address into my much-
Tippexed, crossed out, almost indecipherable address
book. 'Don't *ever*,' she admonished, 'use anything but
a pencil to fill in your address book.' And I never
have.

Felicity Green
Journalist

RENEWABLE

A loose-leaf diary has the advantage that when you renew the engagement part each year the names and addresses stay put. (Keep it in your pocket. Filofaxes and electronic organizers are for women with handbags and men with briefcases.)

The Rt. Hon. James Ramsden

BROUGHT TO BOOK

For those who can't be bothered to maintain a diary, keep a record of anything important in an album. These might be letters or newspaper cuttings of personal or contemporary interest, greeting cards, snapshots, quotations, etc. The only necessity is to date the entries, at least by the month and the year. Thus at any time in the future you can recall memories more vividly than from a diary, but just as personally as you can always add your own comments.

Dr Donald Derrick
Dental surgeon

BELT AND BRACES

If you use an electronic personal organizer, back it up with a handwritten list every day, and keep these for ever.

The Lord Birdwood

INSURANCE POLICY

If you have committed your whole life to an electric organizer, you know, of course, that one day you will drop it in the bath. Buy a spare one today and download it tonight.

Judy Finnigan and Richard Madeley
TV presenters, This Morning

24

NOTELETS

Ever since school, where I got the habit, I have written things – facts, speeches, daily schedules – on 3in x 5in/7.5 x 12.75 cm cards. If it doesn't fit on a three by five it is either too obscure to explain or too complicated to do.

Loyd Grossman
TV presenter

UNTIDY

Don't ever tidy your desk – you'll never find anything!

Nicholas Courtney
Writer

HELPLINE

When you buy your first computer be sure that you get it from a dealer who will give some after sales service. The damn things have curious foibles only a technician can understand and instruction books that are written in a language peculiar to themselves. Resist the temptation to get that bargain at a big department store and go for one from the little man round the corner. Ignore this advice if you have children   they will solve all your problems.

Emma Lubbock
Accountant

HANDS ON

The only way I have found to become computer-literate is to wander round the works, clicking into everything. Eventually, all becomes clear – much more so than trying to understand the manual.

David Chambers
Amateur book designer

NOT SO CLEVER

The important thing to remember about computers is that they are even more stupid than you are, and that they are really quite difficult to break.

Dr Alan Borg
Director, Victoria &Albert Museum

FEELING POORLY

It seems ridiculous, but computers are susceptible to viruses which can play havoc and even destroy all your work. They can come in with borrowed or even bought floppy discs and the real trouble is that you can't tell when you've got one until something awful happens. The only certain way to be sure you aren't infected is to buy an anti-virus checker – the most famous one is Doctor Solomon's. If the computer is an essential part of your life this is vital.

Paula Goodale
Image-licensing agent

PLAYING SAFE

If you're having a long session at the computer, save, save and save again. Power cuts, thunderstorms or your three-year-old pulling out the plug can strike at any time and you really need to save every half hour. And at the end of every session put everything on a back-up disc which you keep somewhere else.

Keith Nichols
Scanning operator

KNOW HOW

When 'Are you sure?' or some equivalent message

comes up on your computer screen, always say no. It is probably referring to something quite important.

❖ ❖ ❖

Keep your computer as tidy as you would your desk. Put all out-of-date and unnecessary files in the wastebasket and have a nice neat screen. This will also ensure lots of space in its memory – limited, unlike the human brain – so you will not have the aggravating experience of typing a ten-page letter only to find it has been aborted for lack of space.

Nick Tomlinson
Production manager

TAKE THE PLUNGE

'Don't get it right, get it written' – an adage that has always helped me enormously. Too much time can be spent fretting over getting the first sentence perfect. If you just launch straight in you can get the body of what you want to say down in writing. It's considerably less daunting to go back and edit less-than-perfect text than to spend hours staring at a blank sheet of paper.

Giles Andreae
Cartoonist and children's author

COVER UP

When correcting proofs or typescript, cover the text *below* the line you are reading – a large envelope or piece of cardboard will serve the purpose. This will help you to spot errors which might otherwise have gone unnoticed.

Diana Witherby
Poet

NOTED

Always put a note in a book saying when you got it and how (gift or purchase), and where and when you read it. This makes browsing through your library much more fun.

Dr Alan Borg
Director, Victoria & Albert Museum

ON A ROLL

If you write a lot of letters, stamps in a roll are much easier than books or sheets. The Post Office have them for stamp machines and you can order them.

The Rt. Hon. James Ramsden

TREASURE TROVES

The fax machine is a wonderful invention but to me there is nothing like good old-fashioned letters for that lovely feeling of personal involvement. I'm a widow now and one of my great pleasures is re-reading letters from those I love, knowing that the ink has flowed from their own pen, and the paper has been folded by their own hand.

Rosemary Chester
Retired headmistress

RECORDED DELIVERY

When my daughter moved to New Zealand, both she and I installed fax machines and we correspond enthusiastically, knowing that our letters arrive on the instant. But there's another advantage: the original letters, which we have both kept, form almost day-to-day diaries of news and views which might otherwise have been lost in the mists of time.

The Lady Wardington

POSTCARDS

With faxes, e-mail, mobile telephones and fast, complicated living, the simple art of letter-writing has become an event of the past – but I always keep some special postcards to send to friends from time to time during the year. A fond letter may require too much time, but a warm postcard can bring a personal message which can be kept for ever as a memento of friendship, and may cheer a dull day when re-read years later.

Anna Massey
Actress

TOO BLUE

Writing a letter to be faxed, never use a blue ballpoint pen or a pencil. If you do, the chances are it will arrive faint and illegible at the other end.

Mary Roberts
Secretary, Katharine House Hospice

LITTLE AND OFTEN

If you write to a friend only once a year you can find very little of importance to say. If you write once a month there seems to be masses of news. In fact, the more often you write, the more you will find to talk about. And this goes for frequent telephone calls too.

Mrs Keith Kotch

ETIQUETTE AND
ENTERTAINING

Very sorry, can't come. Lie follows by post.

LORD CHARLES BERESFORD

FACE-SAVER

In these days of casual telephone invitations, pitfalls await. Someone asks you, 'Are you free on Friday evening?' You say yes, and then you hear, 'And we thought we'd ask X and Y.' You can't stand X and Y but it is too late to back out. A better approach for the hostess might be 'We are inviting X and Y to dinner next Friday and wonder if you would be free to come too?' This ploy allows time for the invention of a face-saving excuse. I cannot recommend it too highly to would-be hostesses.

Frances Bissell
Cookery writer, The Times

HORRORS

Don't ask people who bore you to dinner. You

probably bore them too. Besides, they might ask you back!

Prue Leith
Food writer and restaurateur

TOGETHERNESS

A close girl friend thinks her new husband is the most amusing man on this planet. You and your husband think he's the biggest bore. When, as you must, you invite them to dinner, ask a husband with a dull wife and sit the Boring Ones together. It can save a lot of trouble and can work wonders.

Laurie Purden
Journalist

ILLUSION

If you've had one of those lazy days when housework has proved just too much, and then, when your husband is about to come home or guests are due to arrive, you get an attack of conscience, seize a can of good, strong-smelling furniture polish and spray it into the air all around the hall. Everyone will think you have been busy with a duster all day, and even 'see' the sheen on the mahogany.

Mrs William Mond

RIGHT PRIORITIES

When guests are arriving in ten minutes and nothing is ready, get yourself, your make-up and party clothes done first. You'll feel much better, as you rush around laying the table and putting the meat in, if you are changed and looking nice.

Mrs John Biffen

PRESENTATION IS EVERYTHING

The key to giving a dinner party on a tight budget is presentation. Make the table look wonderful with the best china, glasses, flowers, etc. and present each dish beautifully. Whatever you're serving will please your guests, although it didn't cost a lot. Of course, conversely, if you serve the best ingredients badly – or give too large helpings (a fatal error) – your party won't be such a success.

Angela Perry
Fundraising consultant

KEEP IT SIMPLE

In a long life of entertaining without domestic help and with children growing up, I have come to realize that food is the least important part of a party. Keep the catering simple – it is far more important to have read the newspaper carefully that day.

Lady Kenny

PILLBOX

When I have friends to stay I always put a little box containing a few aspirin and some indigestion pills (easily identifiable) by the bed. Nothing is worse than waking up in a strange house at two in the morning with a headache or heartburn, and I hope it is a comfort to my guests to know that at least those problems can be alleviated. And I put a champagne cork on the bedside table as well. I tell my guests I believe that if you sleep with one in your hand you will not get cramp.

Mrs Annie Howard

PICTURE HATS

Fit hooks round the edge of a wedding marquee for

ladies to hang their hats on. Not only is it practical but also it is picturesque.

Anna Harvey
Deputy Editor, Vogue

LADYLIKE

My mother always felt that one of the signs of a 'true' lady was the ability to put others at their ease. To this end, she gave me strict – and, I may say, supervised – instructions, from the age of seventeen onwards, to spend the first ten minutes of every party where this consideration was needed most. This could mean effecting introductions, digging out wallflowers, sitting on the sofa with Granny or chatting to an uncomfortable fourteen-year-old. This lesson has influenced my behaviour and attitude all my life – indeed I am quite famous for introducing best friends to one another, though I haven't managed sisters yet.

The Lady Edmondstone

GETTING TO KNOW YOU

You should always introduce a gentleman to a lady. For instance, 'Jim, you don't know my wife', is terrible to hear; 'Darling, you don't know Jim', is what you should say.

Sir Hardy Amies
Fashion designer

REST ASSURED

If you are feeling insecure, remember that everybody, no matter how gloriously confident they appear, also suffers from feelings of insecurity over something. And if they don't, then they really *do* have problems.

The Lady Chichester

SOON FORGOT

Should you put your foot in it socially by inept speech or behaviour, remember that everyone else is far too busy thinking about themselves to attend much to you or to keep it in their minds for long.

The Lord Quinton

TIED

When you are invited to a house for the first time you must wear a tie.

Sir Hardy Amies
Fashion designer

WASTE NOT

Do try not to leave good wine standing in your glass when you leave your host's table. It's not only rather rude – it's an expensive waste.

Basil Phillips

ROYAL RULES

We recently received an invitation to a grand dinner party, at the bottom of which was written 'Balmoral rules will apply'. Research revealed that this meant that the guests would be expected to talk to their right-hand neighbour for the first course, turn to the other side for the next and so on through the meal. A good plan, though we thought it unusual to have it stipulated before we had even arrived. Incidentally, we learnt from further research that it is not necessarily applied at Balmoral.

The Lady Saye and Sele

SOCIAL GRACES

The prospect of a large dinner party can be daunting, to say the least, to those of a shy disposition, but this advice from my parents, who spent their life in the diplomatic service, might help:

Have at least three topics of conversation ready before you sit down.

Let the other person do the talking.

The Lady Elton

A B C

Play the alphabet game if you're really stuck for conversation; you will amuse yourself, if no one else. For example, What do you think of Armadillos? Have you been to Barbados? Are you a good Cook? What are your views on Dictators? I once got quite far up the alphabet – but it was a desperate measure. Warning: it is preferable for your neighbour not to discover what you are up to.

Mary Sheepshanks
Author

THE PERFECT ANSWER

Making conversation is difficult enough at the best of times, but if you are deaf, or even a little hard of hearing, it can be a nightmare. I have discovered that nine times out of ten a perfectly adequate response to almost every remark is 'Exactly', said with enthusiasm.

Timothy Sergison-Brooke

TO THE POINT

If someone goes on at great length about a dull subject about which you have no opinion but are expected to say something, nod slowly and say, 'Up to a point, up to a point.' No one will ever ask you which point.

The Rt. Hon. Sir Edward Heath, MP

IT'S THE WAY YOU SAY IT

If someone says, 'Can I pick your brains?' the reaction is usually pretty negative, but even hard-
ened operators have been known to soften when
approached with, 'May I have your advice?' I can't
count the number of times I have used this idea,
gleaned from Shirley Conran's *Superwoman*, to
surprisingly good effect.

The Lady Cazalet

DELIBERATE MISTAKES

Never offend anyone by accident.

Katharine Whitehorn
Journalist

FRIENDS AND FOES

One of my grandmother's most helpful axioms was
that 'one should never make an enemy by
accident.' Naturally, she had no objection to
making one on purpose.

Today, people often make the American mistake of
confusing acquaintances with friends. The former
are there to share life's pleasures; only the latter
should be invited to share one's problems.

Julian Fellowes
Actor and film producer

TAKE THE BLAME

My mother used to say that if anyone was rude to
you twice it was your own fault. After the first
insult you should have cut them out of your life.

Lady Maureen Fellowes

PRICELESS

'Please' and 'thank you' cost nothing but are worth their weight in gold.

The Earl of Perth

BREAD AND BUTTER

The longer you leave a thank-you letter, the longer it takes to write.

The Lady Elton

THE RIGHT LETTER

Letters of congratulation should be quick and short. Insincerity should never intrude; if you feel it can't be avoided, don't write the letter. And don't say 'no reply expected'; recipients nearly always want to reply. Incidentally, the first thank-you letter is the one welcomed the most. It needs to be twice as long if it is late.

Sir Martin Jacomb
Chairman, The British Council

TELL ME MORE

Bread-and-butter letters are on the whole – if they come at all – pretty dreary. A host or hostess cannot possibly know how a party (or whatever) has been for each one of their guests, so to recount an incident, a funny moment or interesting conversation with another guest – i.e. the thing that made the occasion great for you – is always much appreciated. In fact, this kind of letter is often followed up by a telephone call from the host, eager to know more.

Angela Huth
Journalist and author

SECOND CHANCE

It's jolly bad luck, in terms of presents and special attention, to have been born on or near Christmas Day. But if you were, why not give yourself – and let it be known – an 'official' birthday at another time, say around the end of June?

June Ducas
Writer and journalist

HEAR IT AGAIN

Before you go to an opera, particularly if you haven't heard it before, get hold of the tape and play it as often as possible beforehand. You will enjoy the whole work so much more.

Mrs J.E.H. Collins

SHOWING UP

The perfect ploy for an opera buff is not to arrive at the theatre until shortly before the interval. This ensures avoiding the boredom of the first half and means you will get the best table in the bar and be on your second bottle of champagne by the time the audience come out. You can then wave, see and be seen by all – the most important aspect of opera-going. You can take your seat for the second half, when you fall asleep, slightly drunk, thankfully missing again the tedium of the performance, and wake up to join in the best bit, the ecstatic applause at the fall of the curtain. With tears coursing down your cheeks ravaged by such pent-up emotion, you mentally (because it's cheaper) cast bouquets upon the stage while clapping wildly – *Bravissimo!*

Madge de Wycke
Art collector

CURTAIN CALLS

I'm such an avid theatre-goer that I'd have to move house if I stored the programmes of all the shows I've seen, but I do like to keep the memorable ones. I make notes of who I went with, what I thought of the production, and who gave particularly good performances. They are great fun to look back on, especially if you find you've spotted someone who later became famous. But unless you have a better memory than mine, do add the date too, as these don't always appear on the programme and are very helpful in settling which-year-what-was-it? arguments.

Ann Stanwell
Artist

FOOD, GLORIOUS FOOD

There was an old person of Dean
Who dined on one pea and one bean.
He said, 'More than that,
Would make me too fat,'
That cautious old person of Dean.

EDWARD LEAR

MORE OR LESS

The longer the menu description, the less you'll get on your plate. If you're hungry, order Fish and Chips rather than Tuna seared in Hazelnut Oil, garnished with Lime, Coriander, Lemon Grass and Ginger, and served on a Coulis of Mediterranean Tomatoes and Herbs from Provence.

Shirley Lowe
Writer

CRISPY DUCK

If you want the skin of your roast duck to be really crisp, dunk the whole bird in a pan of boiling water for twenty seconds, pat it dry and then roast it in the usual way. Perfect results every time guaranteed.

The Hon. Mrs Pease

WRAP IT UP

Have you tried cooking a chicken in a J-cloth? Melt some butter in a saucepan and soak the J-cloth in it. Then take a chicken prepared in the usual way for roasting and swathe it in the cloth, covering it completely. Roast it in a hot oven and after a short rest unwrap it. You will find the skin brown and crispy, the flesh succulent and the oven unspattered. You can even wash the J-cloth and use it again. If you don't have a J-cloth, a strip of muslin will work just as well.

Theresa Petrie
Management consultant

GAME GAMBIT

Unless you're a dedicated pheasant eater, a seasonal glut can be a mixed blessing, especially if you're the one who has to do the plucking. I've become quite ruthless and cut out the really plump breasts, feathers and all, with a very sharp knife. They can then be easily skinned and put in the freezer, ready to be cooked whenever needed.

The Hon. Mrs Kim Fraser

SOFTENING UP

A cheat's way to soften stewing steak for a casserole (or mince for a lasagna) is to put it, floured and seasoned, into a pan with browned onions and then add a little milk. Carry on cooking until the milk is absorbed and follow with wine, stock or whatever.

Colin McDowell
Fashion historian

JUST A SPOONFUL

A spoonful of Marmite will enhance the flavour of any dish, and is guaranteed to set your table guessing if conversation flags.

Lynne Truss
Writer and novelist

JUST A DASH

A dash of red Thai curry sauce in almost any dish will give it *'je ne sais quoi'*.

Mrs George Rodwell

JUST A DROP

A few drops of anchovy essence will boost a stew. It doesn't make it taste fishy, just brings out the flavour.

John Martin Robinson
Archivist, Arundel Castle

SLICED JACKETS

I discovered this way of cooking a jacket potato by chance when I was in a hurry, and it is wonderful. I cut it across from one side to the other, in half-inch-wide slices, making sure not to cut to the very bottom each time. I baked it in the oven in the usual way and it came out like a splayed-out toast-rack, the sliced skin crispy and lots of room to put masses of butter in the cracks.

Mrs Charles Shepley-Cuthbert

HOT POTATO

Turn simple roast potatoes into a gourmet's delight by dusting them with mustard powder halfway through the cooking time. Very special and so very easy.

Dame Jane Whiteley

TOPS AND TAILS

Bought packets of French beans can be topped and tailed in moments without removing them from the bag. Simply knock one end on the work surface to align all the tails and cut through both pack and beans in one go. Repeat this action with the other end of the pack. All done!

Anna Harvey
Deputy editor, Vogue

BEAN TIME

To save moments when every second counts, open baked bean tins upside down. That way the whole contents plop out with no need to scrape out the beans left behind. And if it opens with a ring-pull, store the tin upside down.

Mrs Bill Tiley

PERFECTION

I test any hotel I stay in by ordering scrambled egg for my first breakfast. How few pass. I have had to face everything from tasteless custard to a sort of dry yellow pebble-dash when what is needed is an effect that the French call *baveuse* – moist without being runny, and straight off a moderate heat.

I make perfect scrambled egg. I melt some butter in a saucepan with a dessertspoon of top of the milk and seasoning to taste. I drop in the egg and mix it in with a large fork, then place over a moderate heat and stir gently with a spoon. Before it is quite ready I switch off the heat and a moment later turn the delicious mixture on to a piece of toast. Perfection – and a clean saucepan.

Michael Denison
Actor

EGGS-ACTLY

A recipe my dear old mother gave me for those frequent evenings when you can't think what to give your returning-home-from-work husband for his supper: 'Give the bugger an egg,' she used to say.

The Lady Cudlipp

SHELL OUT

Quails' eggs and celery salt are synonymous with summer picnics at Ascot, Henley and the Guards Polo. A quick way to peel them is to put them, straight after hard boiling, in the deep freeze for five to ten minutes. The egg slightly shrinks, making it much easier to remove the shell.

Suzanne Kinnear
Actress

SAUCY

Any steamed, baked or boiled fish will be transformed into a delicious dish by the addition of this sauce. Buy one container (10 fl. oz/300ml) of crème fraîche from a supermarket or wherever. It has to be crème fraîche because it is slightly sour. Put in a pan over a very, very low heat and watch it melt, at which point mix in two dessertspoons of mustard – preferably French (English is too strong). Then just pour the sauce over the fish. If you want to mix herbs with it, experiment with parsley, chervil or dill.

Carmen Callil
Editor and publisher

SIMPLY DELICIOUS

This is an invaluable recipe for a really simple and delicious sauce. Roughly chop some ripe plum tomatoes and simmer with white wine (a pint of white wine to a pound of tomatoes) for about half an hour. Rub through a sieve, add some seasoning, and there you have it. If you feel inclined you could add a knob of butter, cream or herbs, according to the dish with which you are serving it.

Steven Saunders
TV cook and restaurateur

FRESH AND FAST

A quick way to make delicious tomato soup without skinning and deseeding is to cut the tomatoes in quarters, throw them into a saucepan with stock to cover and a bunch of whatever fresh herbs you have to hand. Simmer for fifteen minutes, then press the tomatoes through a wire sieve leaving skins, seeds and herbs behind. Season with freshly milled pepper and salt, plus a smidgen of brown sugar. Serve with or without a spoonful of cream. Also makes great chilled tomato juice.

Anne Gregg
Journalist and broadcaster

WELL DRESSED

Here's a fresh and original dressing. To the juice of a tangerine add the juice of half a lemon, a teaspoonful of French mustard, a good dessertspoonful of honey, and salt and pepper. Mix well together and add enough olive oil to give a nice pouring consistency. Store in a bottle, and shake vigorously before pouring over a salad. A handful of chopped mint thrown in at the last minute can add to the flavour.

Sylvia Winterbottom
Computer programmer

45

CHEESE DIP

I find it useful to keep a box of grated cheese in the deep freeze, as it saves time and trouble whenever you want to sprinkle some cheese on a dish you are about to put in the oven or under the grill.

Mrs John Major
Biographer

KITCHEN TRICKS

A little thin stock on top of a thickened gravy prevents a skin from forming. Warm milk on top of custard performs the same function – and mashed potato will keep white and fluffy if a milk topping is whisked in at the last minute.

❖ ❖ ❖

I think most people know that if you put sloes, bagged, into the freezer for three days and then defrost them, they will be perfect for making sloe gin without the laborious business of piercing each one by hand. But few people seem to know that exactly the same treatment (bagging, freezing, defrosting) makes it far easier to put apples, pears and other hard fruits through a fruit press to make fresh juices.

Mrs Neil Hunter

OIL CUBES

Freeze extra virgin olive oil in ice trays, uncovered, and add the cubes to gazpacho just before serving, instead of ice cubes.

Sue Laurence
Food writer

CHOP NOT

To freeze curly parsley, pick off the heads and place in small plastic bags. Seal tightly, leaving plenty of air in the bag. Just before use, take out of the freezer and lay the bag on a chopping board. Bash two or three times with a rolling pin, whereupon the parsley will shatter into small bits, thus doing away with any need to chop.

Frances Smith
Herb and salad supplier

ROLL UP, ROLL UP

When parsley is plentiful I buy a large quantity and chop it all. Then I lay it on a sheet of cling film, pack it firmly together, roll it into a long sausage and freeze it. Whenever I need the herb for garnish or flavouring through the winter I simply slice off the required amount and pop the rest back in the freezer.

The Hon Mrs Petrie

FLAT OUT

To dry bay leaves so that they stay flat for easy storage in jars etc., lay them between the pages of an old telephone directory and leave in a warm place for a week or two.

Frances Smith
Herb and salad supplier

PEEL OFF

To peel individual cloves of garlic cleanly and easily, place the clove on a chopping board, hold the blade of a knife flat across the garlic and give the blade a firm hit with your hand. The skin will come away easily – of the garlic, not your hand!

Jo Cornley
Director of Administration and Finance,
Katharine House Hospice

CURDLE CURE

Making really rich custard with eggs can be tricky; it so quickly curdles if it is overcooked. It is possible to save it if you pour it into a large bottle and shake it hard, as you would a cocktail.

Albert Roux
Chef and restaurateur

EGG WISE

A pinch of cream of tartar will stabilize a whipped egg white. And, although you may know that egg whites will keep in the freezer for at least a year, did you know you can safely refreeze them?

Beth Williams
Caterer

CLUB PUD

When I dine at the Garrick my favourite pudding is ice cream served with stem ginger, liberally sprinkled with freshly ground black pepper and topped with a measure of whisky. Definitely to be recommended as a way to serve ice cream.

Hon. Sir John Owen

BRING OUT THE FLAVOUR

Strawberries are best kept in the fridge, but if eaten ice-cold they lose their flavour. I pop mine into the microwave for half a minute before bringing them to the table, serving them just lukewarm. Like this they need hardly any sugar, just cream.

Mrs Miguel Ferrer

COLD STORE

Always store apples in a perforated plastic bag in

the refrigerator as they soften ten times faster at room temperature.

Mary Kilmartin
Apple grower, New Zealand

SNAPPY TRICKS

Brandy-snap baskets are a fiddle to make and bought ones are so obviously not home-made. I have discovered that if you pop bought 'curled' ones into the oven for a few minutes they will unroll and lie flat. Quickly take them out and place each one over an upturned teacup or small tumbler and when they cool they will fool anyone into thinking you have spent hours over a hot stove.

Vernon Russell-Smith
Garden designer

UPSIDE-DOWN CAKE

It is difficult – well nigh impossible – to put a freshly baked and decorated sponge cake into a tin. But if you put the cake on to the lid and place the tin over it the problem is solved. Remember, though, to label the tin clearly so that a well-meaning family member doesn't turn it the right way up.

Mrs Mary Tolley

FRESH PLEASURES

Don't spend time eating stale bread or you will never enjoy the pleasures of fresh bakery. Remember, there are always the birds!

Judy Light
Chinese herbalist

FROZEN ASSETS

A stress-free way to butter bread for sandwiches is to use a sliced loaf straight from the freezer. Because the slices are firm, the butter won't need much softening (a time-saver, this) and spreads without tearing the slices, which won't take long to thaw. Then they can be assembled in the usual way.

Susan Imre
Journalist

WHO'S FOR TENNIS?

It seems such a waste to throw away old tennis-ball tins: they are so airtight. In fact, they are perfect for storing spaghetti – and if they have a faintly rubbery smell, get rid of it by sprinkling a little (unused!) cat litter in and leaving for a day or two.

Mrs Gerhard Bulle

SHARP PRACTICE

Make friends with your butcher, not just for good meat: he'll also sharpen your knives for you.

Clarissa Dickson Wright
Food writer and TV personality

AGA LOVERS ONLY

I can't cook on anything but my Aga, which presents a serious problem in the heat of the summer – but now I've solved the difficulty. I turn it right down and cover it with a couple of fire blankets, taking care not to cover the flue or the air intake. The heat is thus contained, so that the kitchen isn't tropical, and when I need to cook I simply take the covers off.

Mrs Charles Shepley-Cuthbert

FISH FLAVOURS

We always poach quenelles in fish stock. It gives then much more flavour than when they are cooked in water.

Carmen Lleõ
Professional cook

UNDERCOVER

Don't just hope that what you have put into the microwave will not burst and splash all over the inside, making at least ten minutes' extra work – COVER IT.

The Countess of Minto

QUICK QUICK COUS COUS

Cook cous cous in the microwave. After soaking it in the usual way, two minutes on high should cook enough for four people to perfection.

Sophie Page
Student

CHEERS!

Fill every glass, for wine inspires us
and fires us
With courage, love and joy.

JOHN GAY

SERIOUSLY DRY MARTINI

Take a large bottle of gin. Unscrew the cap and fill
the little space between the top of the gin and the
top of the bottle with vermouth. Replace the cap
and put in the freezer for three days. Consume with
care.

The Lord Quinton

THE VIRTUES OF WHISKY

Whisky sloweth age and strengtheneth youth; it
helpeth digestion and cutteth the phlegm; it
abolisheth melancholie and lighteneth the mynd;
it puffeth away ventositie, keepeth the head from
whirling and eyes from dazzling. It stoppeth the
teeth from chattering and the stomach from wom-
blying, the sinews from shrinking and the bones
from aching. It is indeed a sovereign liquor … *if it
be orderlie taken.*

Ben Yeats Brown,
quoting from speech heard at the Distillers' Co. AGM

52

SAVING

Don't serve pale whisky – guests always help themselves to more!

Sir Adam Butler

DROPS IN THE BOTTLE

Pour a bottle of vodka over half a pound of pear drops and leave until all the sweets have dissolved. Bottle the resulting pink, slightly oily, liquor and drink as an after-dinner liqueur. It is delicious.

Nick Morrison
Hospital porter

CATCH A THIEF

If, heaven forbid, you think that someone may be nipping your spirits while you are away, you can make sure by marking the level of the drink on the bottle. But, so that it isn't obvious, turn the bottle upside down before you make the mark. Then you will know whether or not the booze has gone – but not, of course, who the culprit is.

Anon. by request

INSTANT WARMTH

If red wine is served cold it can be very disappointing, but what can you do if guests arrive unexpectedly or you just haven't had time to get it to a pleasant room temperature? You take off the metal round the top, put the bottle – cork intact – into the microwave and give it twenty seconds on full power. A winner every time.

Geoffrey Flanders
Hairstylist

CHAMBRÉ

In the rationing periods during and after the last war it was difficult to buy wine, good or ordinary. A knowledgeable friend told me that, when serving a bottle of *very* ordinary red wine, one should open it two or three hours in advance and, if desperate, add a little warm water to the opened bottle.

Lady Barbirolli

PASS THE PORT

What can you do with the dregs left in the bottom of that good bottle of port? Easy. Pour them over vanilla ice cream. Delicious.

Hugh Bett
Antiquarian bookseller

QUICK FIX

When you reach the last bit of wine in a bottle, pour it into an ice tray and put it in the freezer. Then, when you need a little wine for a stew, soup or sauce, simply pop in a cube.

Brian Braithwaite
Magazine consultant

WELL SAVED

If you want to drink only half a bottle of wine, immediately on opening pour half into an empty half bottle and cork it so that no air gets in. That way you can keep the recorked half for many days and feel thoroughly virtuous.

The best fancy gadget for saving wine is a Wine-saver, which pumps nitrogen and carbon dioxide into the bottle to replace the air. Vacuum pump gadgets work quite well with cheaper wines, but can also pump out some of the aromas and flavours of better ones.

Charlotte Lessing
Wine and travel writer

ONE BY ONE

For every glass of wine you drink, take one of water alongside. That way you won't get dehydrated or headachy. This is particularly important with champagne or sparkling wines, which have a fast line to the bloodstream.

Charles Whitfield
Master of wine

CHEESE TIME

The French offer cheese after the main course, before the pudding. This they do because they think the cheese helps to digest the meat. I like cheese before the pudding because I can continue with red wine, which is hateful with pudding. Cheese must be served after the pudding if you are passing port.

Sir Hardy Amies
Fashion designer

DEFENSIVE ACTION

If you are going out for what you expect to be a heavy alcoholic evening and you want to keep a clear head, drink a pint of milk before you go.

The Lord Cobbold

STONED

Beware exotic drinks in stone bottles. They may look enticing, but if the bottles haven't been glazed properly on the inside, some of the alcohol will have evaporated into the stone and they will be half empty.

John Goss
Antiquarian map specialist

SLEEP EASY

The perfect after-dinner *digestif* is a '*canarino*'. The Italians know all about it. Simply infuse a generous whirl of lemon peel in hot water, add a little sugar if you have a sweet tooth and sip after a meal or before you go to bed. A peaceful night will surely follow.

Charles Pierce
Director, Pierpont Morgan Library, New York

JUICY

Freeze lemon juice and grated rind in plastic ice trays. Then you will always have the juice to hand when you are in a hurry.

Mrs Michael Howard

INSTANT CAPPUCCINO

No need for a special cappuccino machine. Make it this way. Heat some milk in the microwave for a few minutes, then pour it into your (empty) cafetière. Push the plunger up and down a few times, and the milk will froth up. Pour this on to the top of a cup of coffee and you will find it indistinguishable from the real thing.

John Falloon
Former Minister of Agriculture, New Zealand

LOVE AND MARRIAGE

The deep, deep peace of the double bed, after the hurly burly of the chaise-longue.

Mrs Patrick Campbell

TOGETHERNESS

We are each of us angels with only one wing, and we can only fly by embracing one another.

Rula Lenska
Actress

TELLING

Politeness in a relationship is vital and so, too, in my view, is letting the other person know how much you like or love them. One always feels happier and more relaxed to know one is liked and loved.

Dulcie Grey
Actress

WILD

Approach love and cooking with reckless abandon.

June Smith
Katharine House Bereavement Team

MAKE IT UP

If you have angry words with your loved one, be sure never to let your head hit the pillow at night without making up.

Rula Lenska
Actress

LIVING IN HOPE

The best remedy for compulsive nail-biters is to fall in love with a romantic man who wants to kiss your hand.

Mrs Francisco Ramirez

CHECKMATE

House rule to be established as soon as your teenager reaches the age of consent: there is room for only one couple in any household – and that is going to be you!

Elisabeth Luard
Author

RELATIVE DISTANCES

Always keep a hundred miles between you and your relations.

The Lady Brownlow

WHERE THERE'S A WILL

A really unusual but exceedingly constructive

wedding present would be a will. All newly weds should have one, and in any event marriage automatically revokes an earlier will. Persuade the happy couple to see their solicitor on the promise that you will pay when they have given him their instructions. And tell them to make sure that someone knows where the will is.

Anthony Tahourdin
Solicitor

MAN PROPOSES

When a man proposes marriage, think carefully before you refuse him. Twenty-five per cent of his motivation will be love for you and seventy-five because he wants to get married. Turn him down and within a year he will almost certainly have married someone else.

Mrs Julian Fellowes

HONEYMOONS

Three good rules for a happy honeymoon:

a) Avoid places where either of you have been before (especially with an ex).

b) Better to choose somewhere really special for a week and live like royalty than stretch your money over two weeks on a less memorable holiday.

c) On two-centre honeymoons leave the best to last, since most couples are so tired after their wedding they can hardly remember the first few days anyway.

Lucy Hone
Author, The Good Honeymoon Guide

GET AWAY

If you want to avoid having your car festooned with old boots and embarrasing slogans when you drive away from your wedding reception, hide it somewhere near and get a trusted friend to take you to it when you go away.

Mrs Julian Grove

SLOW BOAT TO CHINA

We decided that we didn't want a party or presents for our 20th (china) wedding anniversary, but we did want to celebrate it in a very special way, so we went on holiday to China.

Ken Hall
Publisher

LOVING SECRET

One of the great secrets of a happy marriage is to have a second honeymoon every year. I don't mean a 'holiday' when you take the children or when you have friends with you all the time. Even if you only snatch a weekend, go somewhere quiet where you are alone. The most important thing is to have good lunches and make love in the afternoon as you did on your honeymoon. Men are at their best at this time and your husband will feel masculine, romantic and in love with you all over again.

Dame Barbara Cartland
Novelist

RECIPE FOR HAPPINESS

My grandmother said that there were three in-gredients which go together to make a successful marriage: love, money and a sense of humour. She said that any two of these were enough to make a good marriage but only one was not enough.

James Price, QC

BABY BREAK

My obstetrician was insistent that my husband and I should have a weekend away from our baby within six months of the birth. This would not only be extremely good for us but also prove to me that my baby would survive without me. We followed his advice, left baby with a most un-suitable-looking woman, had a wonderful time and returned refreshed to a perfectly healthy child.

Barbara Pierce
New York real estate agent

SIMPLE ARITHMATIC?

Une fille, bonne fille;
Deux filles, assez de filles;
Trois filles, trop de filles;
Quatre filles et la mère,
Cinque diables pour le père.

The Rt. Hon. James Ramsden

CONSERVATION

Don't make love to your wife in the morning in case something better turns up in the course of the day.

Geoffrey Ivon Jones

CONFINEMENT

You must keep your husband so poor that he can't afford to walk out of the front door, and so tired that he can't jump over the back fence.

Anonymous Australian lady

HARD WORK

Tottering into the house after a long, hard day at the office, remember that she thinks she has had as hard a day as you know you have had.

Sir Adam Butler

KEEP OUT

Never interfere when friends or relations are having an argument. You will end up with both parties arguing with you.

Baroness Robson of Kidlington

FRIENDSHIP

If you see your best friend's face at every crisis,

If you hear your best friend's laughter through the wall,

If she's next door giving succour to your boyfriend,

P'raps she's not your best friend after all!

Eden Phillips
from his Alfie, the Musical

CHILDREN AND ANIMALS

Men are generally more careful of the breed of their horses and dogs than of their children.

WILLIAM PENN

WHO'S COUNTING?

It's easier to have lots of children who watch out and babysit for each other than one or two who have to be cared for and amused by you. As for men, who wouldn't rather nestle at home with one good man than date dozens of them?

Shirley Lowe
Writer

BONDING

Having a child frees one from any desire to criticize other people's children. Across barriers of age, rank, nationality and politics, the experience of parenting forms a bond of exhausted sympathy.

The Duchess of Marlborough

TELLING TALES

Those of us fortunate enough to have adopted children know the importance of telling them at the earliest possible moment that they are adopted. But it isn't easy for the adoptive mother to impart this knowledge. I knew I would find it very difficult to tell my first adopted child, so I practised on her when she was just a tiny baby. I told her all about Daddy and me so wanting a baby, and how we couldn't have one, and then how her Mummy came along and gave her to us because she wanted her to have all the things she couldn't give her. By the time Lucy was old enough to understand – about two – I was comfortable with the telling and she enjoyed the story. Of course, when she was older, I went into more down-to-earth detail.

The Lady Wardington

BIRTHDAY

Having just had my first baby, the best tip I can give to expectant mothers is to have an epidural.

Mrs Imran Khan

IN THE TEETH

When your baby reaches the stage of wanting to keep rolling over on the changing mat so that it becomes impossible to change his nappy, try putting a rattle or favourite toy in *your* mouth and it will distract him for long enough to complete the manoeuvre.

Annabel Croft
TV presenter and former tennis player

MUSH

To prepare baby's food in advance, fill ice-cube

trays with same, then, when your infant is hungry, all you have to do is pop out a couple of cubes, warm them up and – hey presto – dinner is ready. Very economical too, as there is no waste of time, food or effort.

Senora Josephina Ferrer Frogley de Soler

ON THE LINE

If your mother-in-law doesn't approve of disposable nappies, buy half-a-dozen proper ones – or, better still, beg some tired ones from a friend – and hang them on the clothes line when you know she's coming to see you.

Ann Morrison
Former nanny

BE GRATEFUL

I had a wonderful Australian au pair when the children were small. When I was bemoaning to a friend the fact that she could stay only three more weeks, 'Enjoy every moment of her help and do your worrying when she's gone,' was my wise friend's reply, and I did just that.

Barbara Pierce
New York real estate agent

ROOM FOR NEGOTIATION

Make your children help in the house, garden, or wherever by arranging a work rota, and then let them negotiate their own programme of swapping duties. If not, it's always 'not my turn'.

Charlotte Lessing
Food and travel writer

HOLD 'EM DOWN

To keep young children in their seats at mealtimes, try establishing a routine that the first child to get off its chair (unasked) will have to do some dreary chore such as loading the dishwasher.

The Lady Somerleyton

RIGHTS ISSUE

I tell my grandchildren that everyone has 'rights', but that the more rights a person has, the more responsibilities.

Peter Burnham
Interior designer

SORRY

Never be afraid to apologize to a young child.

Mary Sheepshanks
Author

FAMILY LIKENESS

When your children are young, instead of trying to make them be like you, try to be like them, because it is certain they are much nicer than you are.

Lord Patrick Beresford

SOFTLY, SOFTLY

Whispering works wonders with an angry child. Simply whisper gently into his ear and he will stop crying to hear what you are saying. This is also 100 per cent effective on husbands.

Lady Dashwood

WALKIES

Small children and their adults benefit enormously from an afternoon walk. The immediate result is an appetite for tea and readiness for bedtime; the long-term effect is that when the young grow up they say how much they loved the ritual and remember the simple pleasure with great affection.

The Countess of Minto

LOST IN A CROWD

Small children who get lost in a crowd are often so bewildered that they can't remember who they are. One way round the problem when going on an expedition is to get them to wear one of those plastic identity tubes – the kind you buy in pet shops – with their name, address and telephone number on it. The details can easily be altered when they're on holiday or staying away from home.

Bridget Mason
Postmistress

BLOWN AWAY

Relocate all possible crises out of doors as soon as possible. A good example of this is a tantrum-wielding child. The switch of acoustics does more than relieve the parents' nerves. Children whose yells quickly dominate the enclosed space of a room are often alarmed by their own omnipotence, but outside, they find themselves in competition with everything else going on, and their sense of right proportion returns as if by magic. If this fails, use the rich variety of outdoor distractions for diversionary tactics, along the lines of 'Do you think that cloud looks like a stegosaurus?' or, less honestly, 'Look at that funny little dog! Oh, bad luck, it just went round the corner.'

Hugh Palmer
Location photographer

KEEP MUM

Don't moan to others about the error of your children's ways. You'll forget about them, but other people won't.

Irene Linden
Volunteer, REACH

WHY WORRY?

Don't agonize over the decisions you make for your children. With hindsight you will inevitably find that they were all wrong.

Janet Cropley
Garden designer

NOT GUILTY

Few parents were either wise enough in the past or thick-skinned enough in the present not to agonize over decisions they made for their children. If you are not one of them, wake up one morning and decide enough is enough and you are not going to feel guilty any more. You can't turn the clock back, so make a conscious decision not to worry about things that happened too long ago to be changed.

Annabel Barnett
Tailoress

PRICELESS

The biggest and best present you can ever give your children is your time and understanding – especially at Christmas.

Moyra Bremner
Author and broadcaster

TIME AND TEMPER

No time spent with your children is ever wasted –

and if you lose your temper with them, apologize immediately. This goes for grown-ups, too.

June Smith
Katharine House Hospice Bereavement Team

JUST IN CASE

To encourage your teenagers to leave home, give them a suitcase on their eighteenth birthday, and a larger one on each subsequent birthday. Eventually they won't be able to get into their room.

Elisabeth Luard
Author

OPEN-HANDED

As your children grow older, hold your hand open to let them try their wings; then keep your hand open, and they will wing back happily and of their own accord. But never close your hand or they will have to struggle to get free.

Mary Sheepshanks
Author

WELL CUSHIONED

When my children were teenagers my sister sent me a cushion from America. It read: 'By the time your children are fit to live with, they're living with someone else.'

The Hon. Mrs James Ogilvy

TRAPPY

I always told my children that to plan one's life is optimistic folly – it's ambushes all the way.

Sir Philip Dowson
President, Royal Academy of Arts

NO DELAY

When flying with young children, each child should be in charge of its own luggage – only an on-flight bag for clothes and a small backpack for toys, etc. If mother and father do likewise there will be no luggage in the hold, and your family will be first away from the airport.

Una Stubbs
Actress

WEIGHING IN

Anyone who has tried to persuade their dog to sit quietly on the scales to check its weight will know this is an impossibility. The way to do it is to get on the scales yourself, note your own weight, pick the dog up, weigh again and reckon the difference.

Tim Rootes
Racehorse breeder

GOOD DOG

A good gun dog will be ruined if he is taken out shooting before he is fifteen or sixteen months old. Let him hear a gun go off and let him retrieve a dummy – or even cold game (never warm) – but he will never be a well-mannered dog if he goes out too young.

Mrs Ivo Reed
Owner of Field Trial Champion, Linksview Jet

DAMAGE LIMITATION

The damage a young puppy can do is beyond measure, and of course one cannot keep an eye on it all the time. Limit the damage by unearthing your children's playpen and contain the puppy in it for periods when you cannot watch over it. With toys and a bowl of water, it will be perfectly happy – especially if you place it somewhere where it can see what is going on around it.

Helen Pease

LEARNING THE HOUSE RULES

There is nothing more annoying to live with than a badly behaved dog, except perhaps a badly behaved child, but in both cases they have to be taught what is expected of them before they can develop their own personalities. A badly behaved dog is usually a bewildered one who has been the butt of an impatient swipe or shout. Time and patience need to be spent explaining house rules from the first moment it becomes a member of the family.

Katie Boyle
TV personality and agony aunt

SAFETY FIRST

When you meet a stray dog show him the back of your fist, with fingers clenched – exactly the opposite of when you give your pony an apple or a Polo on the flat of your hand. This way neither will bite you.

The Rt. Hon. James Ramsden

SICK IT UP

If your dog swallows poison or your sleeping pills rush him to the vet but, before that, push washing soda crystals down his throat, which will make him sick within moments. Failing the washing soda, salt will do.

Michael Whatman
Veterinary surgeon

SECRETS OF OLD AGE

Our tortoise, Timothy, has been in our family for 100 years and is probably 150 years old. Needless to say, loving care and attention is lavished upon him and we *never* put him in a warm place to hibernate. He makes his own arrangements which have stood the test of time, including those long terrible winters of 1947 and 1963. The important thing is to feed a pet tortoise well before the cold weather sets in and then let him get on with it.

The Lord Courtenay

DEODORIZER

Even the most devoted cat-lover will agree that, should the cat make a mistake in the house, the resulting smell is awful and long-lasting. Get round this by rubbing the carpet where the offence has occurred with a cloth dampened with ammonia.

Mrs James Curry

TOP CAT

Always let your cat know who's boss. Buy him a bowl with 'BOSS' printed on it.

Lynne Truss
Writer and novelist

LOOKING AT LIFE

*I long ago came to the conclusion that all life is
6-to-5 against.*

DAMON RUNYON.

PLAY UP

Fate has no idea of fairness. You have to play the
cards she deals you, and it is up to you to make the
most of them.

The Lord Weinstock

TODAY'S THE DAY

Look well to this day! For it is life, the very life of
life. In its brief course lie all the varieties and
realities of your existence: the bliss of growth, the
glory of action, the splendour of beauty. For
yesterday is already a dream and tomorrow is only a
vision; but today, well lived, makes every yesterday
a dream of happiness and every tomorrow a vision
of hope. Look well therefore to this day! Such is
the salutation of the dawn.

June Smith
Katharine House Bereavement Team
quoting Sanskrit, translator unknown

CHAOS THEORY

Life is a messy business. Don't try to tidy it up – the task will always defeat you. Learn to live with the contradictions.

Genista McIntosh
Former chief executive, Royal Opera House

BE POSITIVE

Never ask, 'Why me?' Always, 'Why not me?'

Anne Gregg
Journalist and broadcaster

NO REGRETS

Regretting is a waste of time. I only wish I'd learnt that lesson a lot earlier.

Wendy Dear
Journalist

NOT THE SAME

Differentiate between expectation and hope. Never expect anything but hope for everything.

Tim Horn

PAY UP

Have what you want in life, but pay the price.

Mrs Henry Lumley-Savile
quoting a Jewish saying

PLEASE READ ON

Life is a sequence of chapters, and it is important to know that when one chapter is ending, another will very soon begin.

Mrs Barry Lane

FRACTIONS

I once saw this runic observation chalked on a wall.
It seems to sum up life pretty well: 'Seven-eighths of
everything cannot be seen.'

Robert Robinson
Writer and broadcaster

SUNNY THOUGHT

Seen on a sundial:

In caelo terraque
Pars unius quique

(No verbs in sundial Latin.) Translated it means:

In heaven and on earth
Everything is part of one.

My hint is, if you can find truth in this maxim *by
the light of your own experience* you will find the true
meaning of life.

The Lord Tanlow

A GOOD VIEW

God may see our failures as successes, because our
successes make us clever but our failures make us
wise.

Rabbi Lionel Blue

RUB-A-DUB

Everybody makes mistakes – that's why they put
rubbers on the end of pencils.

Billy Connolly,
quoting his father

WHEN WRONG IS RIGHT

If I'm not making any mistakes, I can be sure that I'm not learning and growing.

Lady Weldon

A QUESTION OF LUCK

Thank God for good luck. Immediately before the fall of Singapore, a Japanese bullet passed through my right arm one inch below the curiously named funny bone. If it had hit the joint, in the circumstances I would certainly have lost my arm: therefore no more cricket, no more golf, and learning to write and type left-handed.

Luck is surely the universal thread that runs through all our lives. So it seems to me fifty-four years on.

E.W. Swanton
Journalist, author and broadcaster

LOOKING UP

I can't do better than quote from Charlotte Brontë: 'I avoid looking forward or backward and try to keep looking upward.'

The Duchess of York

HARD TIMES

My Uncle Willy wrote these lines when he was at prep school, aged nine, in 1919:

> Life is a constant struggle,
> A foothold is hard to find;
> Never look before you
> And never look behind.

Major P. W. F. Arkwright

YESTERDAY, TODAY AND TOMORROW

Cherish the past, adorn the present, work for the future.

Sir Simon Towneley

DO YOUR BEST

Always try your best to do or be what you really want. But if it doesn't happen, just accept that it wasn't meant to be. And move on.

Charlotte Lessing
Wine and travel writer

MOVE ALONG

I firmly believe in the old proverb, 'It's no use crying over spilt milk.' If you can't change what has happened, put it behind you and move on to the next thing.

Sir Ranulph Fiennes

A FAVOURITE PRAYER

God grant me the Courage to change the things I can change, the Serenity to accept those things I cannot change, and the Wisdom to know one from the other.

The Duchess of Norfolk

SMILE

If your face feels like smiling, smile. And if it doesn't, then make it smile. In other words, you will feel a lot better when you smile, even if it is forced. And you will find people will be more receptive and friendly to you.

Rosie Atkins
Editor, Gardens Illustrated

BE HAPPY

Happiness is a decision. At some crucial moment in their lives happy people have chosen to be happy.

The Hon. Mrs Charles Kitchener

GO EASY

Make life easier for yourself and everyone else by being a blessing-counter, not a wishful grumbler.

Lady Barbirolli

FUNNY

Two thoughts: a smile costs you nothing, and never forget your sense of humour (if you have been blessed with one).

Mrs Paddy Ashdown

HA-HA

He who laughs most, lasts longest.

John Treneman
Trustee, RELATE

TIME FOR PLEASURE

After you've worked hard to get what you want, make sure you also take the time to enjoy it.

Roland Klein
Fashion designer

ALPHABETICAL ORDER

'The only place where you will find happiness and success coming before work is in the dictionary.' This is not original but it's jolly well correct.

Noel Edmunds
Entertainer

LURKING EVIL

Deceit is a disease without cure; it can be suppressed but never dismissed. Deceit lurks in the soul only looking for an excuse to be released in order to carry out its grimy work.

The Lord McAlpine of West Green

TO YOURSELF BE TRUE

Pretending to be something we're not (and when young I did it often enough) is sad and foolish. None of us has any control over our roots. We have no need to feel shame and no need to feel pride. Our background can be destructive only when we attempt to hide the truth. It's what we make of ourselves and our lives that matters.

Lynda Lee Potter
Newspaper columnist

LIKE ME OR LUMP IT

Never go out of your way to be liked. Life is much too short and the chances are that if you do so you will be starting off on the wrong terms anyway. Be yourself and let them get on with it.

Brian Widlake
TV presenter

ALL GREEK TO ME

I cannot improve on the ancient Greek axioms 'Nothing to excess' and 'Know yourself'. Plato elaborated on the latter when he said that an unexamined life is not worth living.

Sir Nicholas Goodison
Deputy Chairman, Lloyds TSB

HAPPY MEDIUM

Advice to the young (who will of course ignore it). Never undersell yourself. Modesty is charming but people have a habit of taking you at your word. On the other hand, don't oversell yourself – you'll spend the rest of your life having to prove your claims. For example, if you get a reputation for being a super-cook, you'll never be able to invite friends in to a simple supper – they'll expect the exotic, the new and the complicated. This grows more and more tedious as life goes on.

Norman Painting
Actor

FAIRY TALES

Never believe your own publicity.

Sir Alan Ayckbourn
Playwright

SHUSH

Sir Alec Guinness once said to me, 'One has to learn to keep one's trap shut,' and it struck me then as being very good advice. Not easy to follow, but rather something to aim for.

Tom Courtenay
Actor

KEEP MUM

My mother had a commonplace book and I found the following thoughts in it:

Think what you speak but don't speak all you think. Your thoughts are your own but words once spoken are yours no more.

It's better to keep your mouth shut and be

thought a fool, rather than open it and prove that you are one.

The Lady Wardington

SAY SO

People will forgive anything you do but nothing you say.

David Fellowes

IN THE SPOTLIGHT

The world may be large but the jungle paths are surprisingly narrow, so it's wise to remember that wherever you are and whatever you do you are rarely out of view.

Mrs John Treneman

COMMITMENT

Until one is committed there is hesitancy, the chance to draw back, always ineffectiveness. Concerning all acts of initiative and creation there is one elemental truth, the ignorance of which kills countless ideas and splendid plans: that the moment one definitely commits oneself, then providence moves all ... Whatever you can do or dream you can, begin it. Boldness has genius, power and magic in it. Begin it now.

John Lloyd Morgan
quoting Goethe

BE DARING

It is not because things are difficult that we do not dare. It is because we do not dare that they are difficult.

Rula Lenska
Actress

BONEY

It's no good having your wishbone where your backbone ought to be.

The Marchioness of Salisbury

PLAY THE GAME

My old rugby football coach (who was also my headmaster) used to say that to play rugger successfully one needed to be 'resolute to the point of madness'. Such resolution can be applied to other areas of life.

Neil Gadsby
Administrator, Katharine House Hospice

JUDGEMENT

Always judge a person by the way he or she treats somebody who can be of no use to him or her.

The Lady Brownlow

IN HIS SHOES

I like this old American saying which came my way when I was in Washington. 'Before you judge your neighbour, walk a mile in his moccasins.'

Sir Antony Acland
Provost, Eton College

HIS MASTER'S VOICE

On Sundays my housemaster at Eton would teach his lower boys to recite:

Don't look for the flaws as you go through life,
And even when you find them,
It is wise and kind
To be somewhat blind,
And to look for the virtues behind them.

Sixty years later I find there are still occasions on which I find it beneficial to remind myself of these lines.

The Hon. Hugh Astor

WELL CAUGHT

Every day try to catch out somebody doing something right.

The Lord Birdwood

DON'T SAY IT

Try to avoid using the phrase 'You always …', which can be unintentionally wounding.

Professor Teddy Hall

NOT TOO GOOD

If a halo you would wear
Then wear it with a rakish air:
For nothing so perverts the soul
Than too correct a gloriole.

Mary Sheepshanks
Author

IN PERSPECTIVE

Years ago I came upon a piece of good advice which, just occasionally, I try to follow. Look around in a public place and look at each person in sight and say, 'He or she is much better than I am at a number of things. I am much better at several other things.' Both propositions are virtually always true and help to get one's vanities and complexes into perspective.

The Lord Prentice

SEE-SAW

It always seems that life is about balance. An apparent failing in someone can in other circumstances be their strength.

Edward Hardwick
Actor

EVER AWARE

Try never to get so used to anything beautiful that you can no longer see or hear its beauty or purpose. For instance, it's so easy for known and loved prayers to become automatic, and for love itself to be taken for granted.

Valerie Hobson
Actress

ALABASTER BOXES

Do not keep the alabaster boxes of your love and tenderness sealed up until your friends are dead. Fill their lives with sweetness. Speak approving, cheering words while their ears can hear them, and while their hearts can be thrilled and made happier by them; the kind things you mean to say when they are gone, say before they go. The flowers you mean to send for their coffins, send to brighten their homes before they leave them. If my friends have alabaster boxes laid away full of fragrant perfumes of sympathy and affection, which they intend to break over my dead body, I would rather they bring them out in my weary and troubled hours and open them that I may be refreshed and cheered when I need them. I would rather have a plain coffin without a flower, a funeral without eulogy, than a life without the sweetness of love and sympathy. Let us learn to anoint our friends beforehand for their burial. Post mortem kindness does not cheer the burdened spirit. Flowers on the coffin cast no fragrance over the weary way.

Mrs Alexander Thorneycroft,
quoting a tract, published by S.W. Partridge

INSIGHT

Whatever you try to control ends up controlling you.

Mrs Henry Lumley-Savile

WHAT A WONDERFUL WORLD!

It would be nice if we woke up every morning thinking the world was a beautiful place, and that when we went to bed we would not have had to change our minds. A long shot in today's troubled climate but if we all vowed to do our little bit, the world could be as wonderful as we hoped.

Sir James Saville

ONE FOR THE POT

My favourite motto from my husband's Devon–Torquay pottery collection:

Life is mostly froth and bubble.
Two things stand as stone:
Kindness in another's trouble,
Courage in your own.

Mrs Derek Lidstone

LIMITS

It is as important to live within your wit as it is to live within your income.

Colin Franklin,
quoting Lord Chesterfield

DREAMING

Have a lot of secret life, like Walter Mitty. But *never* try to mix up your imaginary activities with the real things in your life.

Professor John Bayley

DOUBLE TALK

Most of the best thoughts have already been conceived, and Henry David Thoreau's on keeping an open mind strike me as very true. It takes two to speak the truth: one to speak and one to hear.

Roger Cook
Investigative TV journalist

BETTER LEFT UNSAID

An observation by the artist Kay Sage, married to the surrealist Yves Tanguy, caught my eye. 'It is difficult to speak about the things that matter most to you. They are the things that you know to be true. Never try to explain the truth …'

Janet Suzman
Actress

TRUST TO INSTINCT

For me, the way to avoid having regrets later is by trusting your instinct. In my experience, first impressions are always right, so go for it.

Judith Chalmers
Radio and TV presenter

DON'T

Never complain, never explain.

Kate Reardon
Fashion director, Tatler

KEYS TO EXISTENCE

I've always liked this advice from the naughtiest girl in town: 'Try everything once and the fun things twice.' Or what the fattest girl in the class regarded as the key to happiness: 'Think of life as just another ruse to distract you from chocolate.' But what I *really* believe gets you through this crazy old world is: 'If you're here, you might as well give it your best shot.'

Frankie McGowan
Writer and novelist

GOOD LOSER

Never bet more than you can comfortably afford to lose.

Jeffrey Peate
Stud owner

TELL IT TO THE MARINES

It was while I was in the Marines that I recognized the significance of the military expression 'Time spent in reconnaissance is seldom wasted.' What has surprised me is how apt it is in civilian life, whether applied to double-glazing or plumbing, buying a car or bringing up children.

Ian Dear
Writer

A WORD TO THE WISE

I am particularly fond of this little piece of homily by someone called Piet Hein:

Shun advice at any price –
That's what I call good advice!

Brian Braithwaite
Magazine consultant

REGRETS

One regrets one's economies more often than one's
extravagances.

J.E.H. Collins
Banker

SPLASH OUT

There are times when extravagance is sensible and
frugality a complete waste. For instance, if you use
a dab of scent only on special occasions, by the
time the bottle is half empty all the actual perfume
will have evaporated. A hundred daffodil bulbs will
hardly make a show – plant a thousand and revel
in the beauty. Buy a beautiful piece of furniture and
it will soar in value while something mundane will
just keep pace with inflation.

The Lady May

PLAY TAG

'*Tantidem Homerus dormitat*' (Sometimes even
Homer nods off). Not actually a true quotation but
a shortened version of a line from Horace's *Ars
Poetica*. It should be spoken quietly and knowingly
to the world in general but loudly enough for your
target to hear it clearly. Targets can be widely
chosen: the Field Master out hunting who stops at
the fence in front of you; your opponent playing
golf who is a much better player than you but just
sometimes makes a bish shot; I'm told it's a very
useful tag for bridge players. With any luck your
target will ask what it means, in which case your
superiority as a classical scholar will be established.

John Hawkesworth
Film and TV producer and dramatist

DISCRETION

Degrees are like false teeth. You'd rather not be without them but you don't need to flaunt them to the world.

Godfrey Smith
Journalist and writer

SHAKE OUT

Cut down the time devoted to Sunday papers by picking them up, shaking them lightly and reading only the sections that stay in your hand.

Lynne Truss
Writer and novelist

STAY PUT

Never get out of the bath to answer the telephone. It always stops before you get there.

The Lady Hesketh

TIDY UP

Don't put it down, put it away.

Sue Arnold
Journalist

INSTANT ATTENTION

Don't hang around for hours waiting to be served in a department store. If you want quick service, pick something up from the display and walk briskly towards the door. Someone will be at your side, asking if you require assistance, before you've taken ten paces.

Colin McDowell
Fashion historian

FIRST OFF

I waste a great deal of time reading books on management and stress, which is idiotic as I don't manage anybody or anything and I'm much more soporific and relaxed than needing any de-stressing. But I did read a wonderful hint that you should begin each day by doing the thing that you *least* want to do. It might be making a telephone call that you have been putting off, offering an apology, refusing a request, defrosting the fridge, weighing yourself, cleaning the oven or taking up a collection for an unpopular colleague. You will feel so good when you have done what you were dreading that a kind of halo will settle around you and you will achieve much more than usual during the day.

Maeve Binchy
Novelist

PRACTICAL MATTERS

*I want a house that's got over its troubles; I don't
want to spend the rest of my life bringing up a young
and inexperienced house.*

JEROME K. JEROME

MINIMAL CHIC

Remember how spaciously elegant your house/
flat/room looked before you added the furniture and
fittings? I once visited Shirley Conran (pre-
Superwoman) when she was strapped for cash. She
was living in a bare white room with nothing but a
vast mattress plus duvet and a David Hockney palm
tree. A fine example of Early Minimalist Chic.

Shirley Lowe
Writer

GOOD TASTE

Providing you have an 'eye', which is God-given,
Sir Joshua Reynolds' advice that 'Taste does not
come by chance: it is a long and laborious task to
acquire it' is spot on.

Mrs Jean Monro
Interior designer

91

WHERE THE YELLOW WENT

One way to stop white paint from turning yellow is to put a drop of black paint in the pot and mix it well in.

Percy Smith
Decorator

DRIP CATCHER

Stop paint dripping on to your head when you're painting the ceiling, by pushing the brush through a paper plate, securing it with sticky tape.

Jake Peters
Carpenter

HANG-UPS

The best way to store paintbrushes so that the bristles stay soft and pliable is to drill holes through the handles and thread them on to a length of stiff wire. Then all that needs to be done is to suspend the brushes over a suitable container and fill it with enough water to cover the brush head. Make sure that it doesn't touch the base of the can, though, as over time this would distort the shape of the bristles. It also goes without saying that you need to keep the water level topped up.

Ernest Pope
Builder and decorator

GOOD PROPORTIONS

The depth of your pelmet should be one-sixth of the total drop of the curtains. This simple measurement will always give you the right proportions.

Angela Darling
Interior designer

PULL FREE

If the cording system is sticking, spray the back of the curtain track with a very small amount of furniture polish. Then run the curtains backwards and forwards a few times and the problem should be solved.

Angela Darling
Interior designer

THE RIGHT HEIGHT

When picking a partner to help you hang pictures and mirrors – mirrors especially – be sure to choose someone about your own height. If they're shorter, you'll feel like Snow White in the seven dwarfs' cottage, and if they are taller, everything will be, literally, over your head.

Sophie Kotch
Office manager

GET THE PICTURE

To make sure your picture is going to hang exactly where you want it, take a length of really strong wire, and make a hook at one end and a small circle at the other. Now, hook the hook on to the wire on the picture and put a strong pin in the circle. Offer up the picture, hanging from the wire you have constructed and position it as wished, making a small hole with the pin to mark the spot. Take the picture down, measure the length of the wire from hook to pin and then fix your picture hangers that distance from the pin hole. I have found this most useful, particularly when trying to hang a number of pictures in a straight line.

Stirling Moss
Racing driver

SHED A LITTLE LIGHT

If a picture light is too bright – and it is better dim than glaring – pierce tiny holes in a piece of aluminium foil and wrap it round the light bulb. If you think it is not letting enough light through, make more holes until you have achieved the required effect.

Felix Kelly
Artist

CUPBOARD LOVE

The best remedy I know for easing drawers that have started to stick is to rub drawers and runners with the stub of an old candle – any old bit of candle will do.

Mrs Barry Lane

HUSH

Expensive kitchen cupboards close with a quiet thump. If yours snap shut with a bang, stick a strip of self-adhesive draught excluder to the inside of the door, where it hits the jamb.

Peter Groom
Kitchen fitter

NICE AND SPICY

Mothballs do the job they are made for but they smell terrible. To counter this, put whole cloves in the pockets of woollen jackets or in bags with sweaters. Cloves also help to prevent moth damage and have a nice spicy odour.

Lady Dashwood

PEEL OFF

Keep moths out of your cupboards by leaving dried

orange peel on the shelves and in the drawers. They hate the smell and will stay well away.

David Sassoon
Fashion designer

BAG THE BAG

Plastic bags proliferate round me like bees round a honey pot, overflowing from drawers and spilling out of cupboards. At last I have found a way to contain them. I made a tube (from cotton chintz) about 2 ft/0.6 m long with a 10 in/25.5 cm diameter, gathered it on to a drawstring at both ends and added a loop to hang it up by. I stuff my plastic bags in one end and, when needed, pull them out from the other.

Diana Stenson
Producer, Classic FM Gardening Forum

SHINE ON

Maintain a high shine on silver you're not using every day by storing it in airtight plastic bags. Then, when you need it, all you have to do is give it a light polish with a silver-cleaning cloth.

Nicholas Worth
Designer

SPARKLING CLEAN

Pewter and brass can be damaged by constant cleaning. To avoid this, clean first with Autosol (from car accessory shops). Dry completely, and then polish with Renaissance wax – a special micro-crystalline polish which can be bought at antiques fairs and some antique shops.

Paul Carr-Griffin
House steward with the National Trust

BRASSED OFF

To remove the powdery deposit sometimes left after cleaning brass, mix one teaspoonful of washing-up liquid with one teaspoonful of citric acid (obtainable from the wine-making department of Boots) and add 1 pt/0.5 litres of water. Apply thoroughly with a brush and rub off with a soft cloth. Thereafter, when cleaning the brass use an anti-tarnish silver-cleaning cloth. This will give a good shine and leave no residue.

Lady Cooke

BLAZE AWAY

To clean brass blazer buttons (or any other buttons where you want to keep the polish away from the cloth) make a straight cut into the middle of a piece of card, and slot this under the button while you work.

Mrs Keith Kotch

ALL FOR SHOW

An old cavalry trooper once told me, 'If you've no time to do anything else, just polish the toes of your boots.' I apply this to life. No time to cut the grass – just mow a strip round the edge of the lawn. No time to clean the whole car – just wash the bonnet.

Robert Wheatley

SHOE-SHINE GIRL

Even shoe-cleaning brushes need washing every now and then – a mucky job that can all too easily gum up the sink or basin with hard-to-remove bits of old polish. To avoid this, pour warm, soapy water into a watertight plastic bag, and leave the brushes to soak in that for a while. Then just tip out the water and throw away the bits with the bag.

Mrs Jean Appleby

INSIDE OUT

Always wash your cords inside out – it stops the pile from getting rubbed.

Alice Colling
Schoolgirl

UP TIGHT

Do up your bra before you put it in the washing machine – then the hooks won't snag delicate undies and make tiresome holes.

Mrs David Rowlands

ONE FOR THE POT

If you don't want the whole house to reek of paint when you're decorating, put a few drops of vanilla essence in the pot before you start.

Robert Harding
Antiquarian bookseller

SMOKE SCREEN

Try placing a dish of vinegar in a room where people are likely to smoke. It's a great deal better than some of the commercial room-sprays, which often smell worse than what they are designed to hide.

Trish Ingley
Headhunter

NO STREAKING

To clean your spectacles without a streak, use a drop of vinegar or vodka.

Lady Dashwood

SOFT SOAP

Find leftover pieces of old soap, squash them together and throw them in the bin. You will feel a lot better for it.

Lynne Truss
Writer and novelist

EFFORTLESS

The easiest way to clean a glass decanter is to put a Steradent tablet in it, fill it up with warm water and leave it to soak. All stains will disappear.

Mrs Michael Howard

THE STING

If you have port- or wine-stained decanters, all you need to do is to fill them with water, push in some stinging nettles and let them stand for an hour or two, and all the stains will be gone.

The Lord Cobbold

OIL WELL

If the stopper of your decanter gets stuck, try dripping a little olive oil around the rim of the stopper. Leave the decanter in a warm place so that the oil can work its way down and then tap gently, upwards and sideways, with a wooden spoon, repeating until the stopper shifts. (And when it does, pour yourself the drink you will have earned by patience and perseverance.)

Francis Sitwell
Historic-home owner

FREEZING THE CANDLE

Keep candles in the deep freeze – then they never

drip when they're lit, even if they've only been in the freezer for a day.

Mrs Valerie Ross

BURNING THE CANDLE

To remove wax that has dripped on to silver candlesticks, and to avoid scratching, melt it with a hairdryer and wipe it away with a paper towel, which easily absorbs grease.

Mrs Andrew Derrick

LONG LIGHT

When a taper isn't to hand, and you want to light candles in a tall, deep container, fit a match into the end of an uncooked piece of spaghetti and use that.

Lady Dashwood

QUICK TIP

A brown felt-tip pen (from an art shop) proves very useful as a quick touch-up for scratched furniture.

Douglas von Katzer
Hairstylist

SPARKLING WHITE

To get the stains off a white synthetic sink, when all else fails, try rubbing with white fluoride toothpaste.

Mrs Hugo Meynell

CLEAN WITH CUSTARD

For problems such as milk spilt on car carpets or – ultimate horror – liquid from a bag of fish, sprinkle custard powder on the offending area, wait for it to dry and then vacuum. In most cases, this does the trick.

The Earl of Shrewsbury and Talbot

SALT STAINS

If red wine is spilt on the carpet and the usual splash of white wine is not available to pour on it, cover the stains with a thick layer of kitchen salt, leave for an hour, then vacuum. Add another good layer, leave overnight and vacuum again. The result, even on a cream carpet, is very good.

Jane Avenel-Evans
Public relations consultant

EGG NOGG

An egg dropped on the floor makes a daunting mess. If, however, you smother it with salt the whole thing will coagulate and clearing it up will be the work of a moment.

June Zetter
Housekeeper

CATCH THE SPILL

Save the aluminium baking cases that quiches, cheesecakes, etc. are made in and put them under the rings of your cooker to catch the inevitable spills and splashes. I line the bottom of my oven with a sheet of foil, too, and throw it away when it gets too nasty.

Mrs Peter Barker

FAT FREE

Put a couple of slices of bread under the rack in the bottom of the pan when grilling meat. They will absorb the grease and stop it burning – and be easy to throw away.

Barbara Cochrane
Housekeeper

FOILED AGAIN

There is nothing as efficient as a Brillo pad for cleaning and shining saucepans but oh, how nasty they get when they go rusty, which always seems to be after one scrub. Now I have solved this problem. When not in use, wrap the pad in silver foil.

Ruth Brass
Schoolteacher

GOLD STANDARD

After washing china decorated with gold lustre, rub lightly with an old (wet) tea bag. This will maintain the lustre without being harsh on the gold.

Nicholas Worth
Designer

WASH AND WAX

Good antiques take kindly to a once-a-year wash with warm water containing a dash of Fairy Liquid. Dry off thoroughly, then polish the clean surface with a good wax polish — and plenty of elbow grease.

Paul Carr-Griffin
House steward with the National Trust

HANDY

The most versatile tools in your kitchen, easily cleaned and always readily available, are your hands. Use them for kneading and mixing, and especially squeezing meat and pressing fish to see if it is done. Better than any gadget you can buy.

Steven Saunders
TV cook and restaurateur

HAIR OF THE DOG

One of the most effective ways of getting cat and dog hairs off upholstered furniture is to don a dampened rubber glove, and wipe your hand firmly across it. The stray hairs gather into a neat bunch, which makes them easy to pick up and throw away.

Mary White
Beautician

FIRE, FIRE

Keep all your old corks – a handful or so make excellent firelighters.

Michael Mander
Cathedral designer

EGG-BOX FIRELIGHTER

Don't throw away cardboard egg boxes or candle ends – they make the best firelighters ever. Place two pieces of candle in half an egg box under your logs and put a match to the box. The melting wax keeps the boxes burning for long enough to get a good fire going.

Mrs Angela Baldwin
Interior designer

STICK 'EM UP

Always have a roll of Sellotape handy – it will:

a) hem skirts (short term)
b) remove fluff
c) seal envelopes that don't stick
d) deflea cat (gently!)
e) mend fraying iron flex (temporarily).

Rabbi Julia Neuberger

SWITCH

Before you arrange for the man to come to fix the dishwasher, boiler or whatever, make sure it really is broken. It is surprising how often the only problem is that someone has switched off the power!

Jo Cornley
Director of Administration and Finance,
Katharine House Hospice

RIGHT FOR REPAIR

Always have a few pipe-cleaners handy. They are the only things which are soft, strong and pliable, and which you can cut with a knife. Thus they do for many repairs – lost collar studs, cuff links, etc.

The Rt. Hon. James Ramsden

SUPER-CARE

Keeping opened tubes of super-glue in the fridge will stop them drying out.

Reg Chapman
Ironmonger

ROPEY

Have you ever wondered why it is that when you or I attempt to coil a rope it very often twists into a hideous figure of eight, whereas if it is done by an expert – such as a sailor or mountaineer – it invariably makes neat loops. The trick is simple. Ropes, like human beings, are either left-handed or right-handed. If, when holding the rope in one hand and coiling it with the other, you find it is making figures of eight, just swap hands. The result will be perfection.

Lord Patrick Beresford

TIED UP TIGHT

Before tying up a parcel, wet the string. When it dries it will tighten, thus making the parcel more secure.

Roland Klein
Fashion designer

PAIRING

How often are you left with several left-handed rubber gloves? Make them into pairs by turning one inside out.

Jenny Ellison
Physiotherapist

BOTTLED-UP

Collect all those tiresome little 5p pieces in a Dimple Haig bottle and use them to fill the endless stream of charity envelopes that come through the letter box. Painless giving.

Mrs Barry Lane

HIDE AWAY

The best way to hide small pieces of precious jewellery from potential burglars is to put them in an ice-cube tray, fill it with water and freeze it.

Name withheld for obvious reasons

GREEN FINGERS

I have a garden of my own
But so with roses overgrown
And lilies, that you would it guess
To be a little wilderness.

ANDREW MARVELL

WAIT AND SEE

When you move into a house with a mature garden, try to contain yourself with patience and wait for a whole year before making any alterations. Each season may bring surprises and it will be very exciting to see what wonders unfold.

Prue Stannard
Garden designer and advisor

LOOK OUT

Do remember when designing your garden that you will only be in it during the summer months, and for the rest of the year you will mainly see it from your windows. So, when planning, look carefully from the house so that you can relate the design to the views and the main features within the garden.

Robert Adams
Garden designer

DREAMING

The purpose of a garden is to give delight. That it is the only work of art which most of us ever attempt doubles the pleasure it gives – to the creator and (with luck) to the spectator. What's more, it has an annual cycle. The debris of autumn will turn into the brilliance of spring. And this happens year after year after year. I wish that people were like this. Would it not be wonderful if we could sleep throughout the winter and emerge looking nineteen years old next May?

Nigel Nicolson
Author

THE REAL THING

Organic matter, well dug into the garden, is the secret to all succesful gardening. Whether it is vegetable peelings or farmyard manure, it has no substitute. It will retain moisture and goodness in the ground for years after man-made products have wasted away, and, best of all, if you have a well-kept compost heap, it will cost you nothing.

Christopher Brown
Nurseryman and garden designer

HIGH TREES

How high is that tree? Here's how to tell. First be sure the sun is shining and place a stick in the ground next to the tree, then:

1. Measure the length of the stick (a).
2. Measure the length of the shadow of the stick (b).
3. Measure the length of the shadow of the tree (c).

4. The height of the tree (d) is found from the following simple equation:

$d = a \times c/b$ (d equals a multiplied by c divided by b).

The Lord Saye and Sele

LEAFY LEGACY

One of the most satisfying ways of making a mark in the world is to plant a tree. Your own oak, grown from an acorn, will please you for your whole life. But don't waste time. Make sure the acorn is alive and well before you plant it by putting it in a bucket of water. If it floats it's no good.

Lord Oaksey

CARING AND REARING

I cosset my newly planted shrub border as I do my children. Plenty of good food, lots of comfort and an ever-watchful eye for danger and disease. I am hoping that when the shrubs and my daughters are grown-up they will be able to fend for themselves without much trouble to me.

Roddy Llewellyn
Garden designer

DEAD OR ALIVE

A sure-fire way to tell whether a shrub is alive or dead is to scrape a twig or branch with your fingernail. If the wood under the bark is green, all is well. If it's brown, it's had it. Cut back to a living piece or abandon hope if the whole thing is dead.

Helen Morling
Head gardener

WATER TROUGH

Shrubs and trees planted on a slope become dehydrated easily. One way to alleviate this problem is to make a deep indentation behind the plant, which will stop any water running away down the hill.

Justine Millar
Garden design student

GOOD GARDENING

Leaves are with us for longer than flowers, so select first those plants that have attractive foliage.

❖ ❖ ❖

If you have a very rare plant in your garden, be sure to give a portion of it to a friend, lest your own plant should die.

Graham Thomas
Gardens consultant

TAGGED

Be sure always, without fail, to tie a clear, indelible label to every flower, shrub and tree you put in the garden. However well you know its name when you plant it, a year or two later when a friend admires it and asks you what it's called, without the label you will be stumped.

The Rt. Hon. Michael Heseltine, MP

KNOW THEIR PLACE

Keep a record of all the bulbs you plant. Note their names and the date and place of planting. Later add their flowering date, and, after they have flowered, whether they have been left in the ground or lifted and stored. This will make your autumn planting much easier.

We keep the same group of colours in each border each year. For example, white and yellow, white and pink, deep pink with carmine red, scarlet and white. In doing this we avoid clashing colours, although it may be good, somewhere in the garden, to have a medley of colours to surprise.

Rosemary Verey
Garden designer

FORGET THE RULES

Don't be browbeaten by expert gardeners into thinking that there is only one time of the year when you can do certain operations. The chances are that by the time you have discovered when the right time is, you will have missed it. Instead, do the job when you notice it needs doing and when you have time to do it. If you want to dig up a rose bush and move it in July, then do it. Just make sure you water it well and spray it with water for a few days until it stands up again. If it dies, tell yourself it was never up to much anyway.

Alan Titchmarsh
Garden journalist and TV presenter

SOW THE SEED

One sure-fire way to propagate gentians, hellebores and pulsatillas is to harvest the seed when the pods are just about to burst and sow it directly into compost. Don't store it for even a few weeks; sown immediately the germination rate should be terrific.

Christopher Brown
Nurseryman and garden designer

TEASING

The proliferation of container-grown plants has revolutionized the garden centre industry but buyer beware. If you don't tease out the roots of the new purchase and soak them well before planting, it may never be able to take advantage of its new situation and will sit and sulk for years.

Gordon Welburn
Head gardener

WEEDLESS

Follow these instructions and you will eradicate bindweed from your garden.

1. Insert a garden cane into the ground at a forty-five-degree angle beside the offending bindweed and encourage it to grow up and climb round the cane.
2. Take a largish yoghurt pot and cut out the bottom.
3. Put the yoghurt pot, removed-bottom side down, over the bindweed and the cane and push it down until it touches the soil.
4. Push the bindweed down the cane until it is all contained within the pot.
5. Using a small hand-spray of weedkiller, spray liberally, keeping the nozzle inside the pot. (This will avoid the weedkiller going on other plants.)
6. Within a week the bindweed will be receding, and the weedkiller will be penetrating its roots and it will be eradicated for good.
7. Remove the pot but leave the cane just in case the bindweed reappears next year.

Rosemary Alexander
Principal, English Gardening School

FENCE DEFENCE

Harpic poured down the side of a fence will stop your neighbour's columbine invading your garden.

Ruby Nag
Home help

TIME AND MOTION STUDY

I always fill empty milk bottles with cold water and pour it into the flower pots on the front steps before leaving them for the milkman to collect. My trailing petunias have been a picture this year and I never have to make a special journey to water them.

Prunella Scales
Actress

FRUITFUL

It is tempting to leave the last windfall apples lying under the trees for the birds, but by doing so you are courting disaster. The rotting fruit can easily cause disease in the trees. Gather them together in a pile outside the orchard area; the birds will feed on them just as happily and the pile will be gone by early spring.

Daphne Ledward
Garden designer

DIG IN

If you have lots of woody prunings or lopped branches, cut them to 1m/3¼ ft lengths and put them at the bottom of your compost heap or bury them in deep trenches in the vegetable garden, where they will break down slowly and provide nutrition over a long period.

Robert Adams
Garden designer

BADGER BAN

Marauding badgers have been ruining my garden, eating the apples and pears and, worse, digging up the daffodil and tulip bulbs. Now I think I have found a badger repellent: lion's dung, which I spread around the garden perimeter. I got my dung from a local safari park but I am told that it is now possible to buy lion's dung pellets.

Mrs Rafelfinger

ROLL UP, ROLL UP

Should your garden hose get stiff with cold and refuse to coil, attach one end to the hot water tap and run it through, or pour a kettleful of hot water down it. It will quickly become malleable.

Andrew Derrick
Graphic designer

THE KINDEST CUT

Never send loose flowers to people in hospital. Patients are there because they're ill or need to rest. They are not there to moonlight as florists. Also (as when a particularly popular couple produce an heir) even the best private hospitals run out of vases. Send baskets of jasmine, hyacinths or miniature roses.

Jane Procter
Editor, Tatler

TRANSPORTS OF DELIGHT

Here's a way to transport freshly cut flowers. Cut off the top quarter of a 2-litre/½ gallon plastic bottle. Half fill it with water. Wrap the stems of the flowers in newspaper and insert them into the bottle. The newspaper will absorb the water and prevent spills while the bottle is in transit, wedged in a basket.

Derek Collins
Flat agent

HOLD UP

Old hair rollers, tied together in a bunch, make excellent flower holders if placed upright in a vase.

Jenny Jones
Assistant florist

FLOWER POWER

Foxgloves give height and elegance to a flower arrangement and they have the further advantage of helping the other flowers in the vase to live longer. Nasturtiums, on the other hand, are extremely bad in that way. Luckily, one is rarely tempted to use them as decoration. They are wonderful in a salad, though.

Mrs Valerie Ross

WRAPPED

Wrap freshly cut sweet peas loosely in newspaper and leave them for a while. Those little black pollen beetles will drop out of the flowers and can be discarded with the paper before putting the blooms in water.

Liza Goddard
Actress

DRINKERS

Hydrangeas drink through their petals as well as their stems, so two minutes upside down in a bucket of water works wonders.

Jean Abbott
Flower arranger

IFS AND BUTS

In the days of drought the water-butt has become an all-important feature of the garden. But in hot weather the water may become green and evil-smelling. Try curing this with a good dose of charcoal – roughly 8 oz to 1 gallon/226g to 4.5 litres.

Philip Watts
Gardener

POTATO PLANTER

Heathers can survive for a long time without water. One can make a very successful arrangement by pushing their stems into a potato placed in the top of a wine glass.

Rosemary Harroby
Florist

GREAT GAS

Perhaps most people know that a banana will help to ripen an avocado if the two are put together in a polythene bag. Bananas give off a gas that has a ripening effect. By the same token, they will have a similar effect on flowers, so keep a flower arrangement away from a fruit bowl if you want it to last.

The Lord Rotherwick

CLOUDLESS

When arranging flowers in a glass vase, put a tablespoon of bleach in the water. This prevents the water from going cloudy and doesn't seem to do the flowers any harm.

Rosemary Alexander
Principal, English Gardening School

SUCCESS STORIES

The secret of success,
'Tis easy,
And easy to express.
To err, and err
And err again,
But less and less
And less.

ANON.

WHAT YOU WANT

Success can be as much a matter of wanting what you get as getting what you want.

Katharine Whitehorn
Journalist

FOLLOW UP

Aim to be the best and the rest will follow.

Anthea Turner
TV presenter

MAKING DREAMS COME TRUE

If you really want to do something, if you have a dream, you can make it happen by giving it your full commitment. Don't listen to others, who will put up any number of negative barriers – too risky, you haven't got the qualifications, it's too difficult.

There is no such word as 'impossible', and one of the great challenges in life is turning that impossible into the achievable. It's not an easy trail, for it requires a lot of hard work, a lot of what might be perceived as risk in terms of security and jobs in the future, but it can lead to that vital fulfilment of developing and bringing together one's aspirations, abilities and ideals into a more complete whole.

Sir Chris Bonington
Mountaineer

WORK AT IT

Strive to accomplish your ambitions and gain the summit of your abilities. But it is only an achievement if you succeed in this without hurting or harming anyone on your way. Above all, never give up.

Christopher Lee
Actor

NO SUCH WORD AS NO

Never say no to an opportunity. I was a nurse and midwife who had a small talent for writing and I followed every chance that came my way. However scared I was I said 'Yes', working on the principle that I could always go back and confess I had bitten off more than I could chew and then pull out. I knew perfectly well that if I said no to start with, there was no way I could go back and say, 'I've changed my mind and now I'd like to have a go.' The worst that has happened is that I have occasionally made a fool of myself, and the best that has happened is that I've built a portfolio of a career that has given me a lot of fun and happiness.

Claire Rayner
Agony aunt

GOLDEN RULES

a) Get up early.
b) Don't put things off: do them straight away, starting with the one you dread most.
c) Don't learn to type until you're forty-two.
d) Have a very clear vision in your head of what you want to achieve, and check this as you go along, because it will change.
e) Always have a toothbrush with you.
f) Only listen to advice if it's encouraging. You are the only one who can decide what's best, and if you are doing something that's never been done before, that can baffle people and they may try to put you off.

Victoria Wood
Comedienne

OPEN WINDOWS

The window of opportunity probably remains a little ajar all through one's life. It is sensible to squeeze through it whilst the gap is wide enough to do it comfortably. Unlock your dream, whether it is to write a book, study, gain qualifications or become a pig farmer (that's what I did). Don't wait until the window has slammed shut.

The Countess of Minto

LIVE IN THE PRESENT

The ability to 'stick with it' as well as good luck, good timing and hard work are probably the keys to success, but most useful to me, in both my professional and private lives, is the ability to live as fully as possible in the present. In my experience this applies as much to work as to relationships, and although it can be difficult to sustain in a modern society where forward planning is often essential, I have found it to be a key factor in creating a rewarding and fulfilling life.

Christopher Gable
Artistic director, Northern Ballet Theatre

KEEP TO THE ROAD

I have no secret for my success: I think it happened in spite of me. Perhaps that is the secret – not to strive for end-products like money or for 'happiness'. These are all incidental by-products of no real significance in themselves. It is the road of life, the path which must contain all the secrets, not the goal.

The Lord Menuhin

A GOOD GUIDE

In my experience the best guides to success are maxims imparted to us by others, reflected upon and then put into practice over time, as:

(In great matters:) simplify without distorting.
(In business:)   always explain, always apologize.
(In banking:)   remember that it's other
                     people's money.
(In negotiation:)   play your losers first.

Sir Jeremy Morse
Former Chairman of Lloyds Bank

TRICK OF FATE

Opportunism and flexibility, qualities for which I have no great admiration, seem to bring success. You have to make the most of your chances, but the people I personally admire most are those who resist such compromise with the world.

Richard Baker
Broadcaster and author

SOUNDS EASY

Try hard and, better still, have a rich father – not that I did.

Frank Muir
Writer and broadcaster

PREPARE FOR THE WORST

As a firm believer in Sod's Law I've always worried my way to success in my work. That way, I suppose, one is inclined to think, plan and work harder. On my way to an appointment I build in time not only for a delayed train but for a full-scale nuclear holocaust during the journey. At present, in preparation for around fifty seconds' video filming of sheep next week, I'm spending so much time standing in fields studying them that they are beginning to worry, which is a pity because I'm a vegetarian.

Never believe 'it will all come out right on the night.' It won't. Fate awaits, ready to clobber your project with a sack of bricks unless you remember your Boy Scout (in my case Brownie) training: *be prepared*!

Audrey Eyton
Author of The F-Plan Diet

ALL CHANGE

Don't play safe, and don't be afraid of changing your whole working life in midstream. If you're not really comfortable in your job, leave it and try something else. In life one very seldom finds oneself regretting the sins of commission; it's the sins of omission – not having done something when you could have done it – that rankle for ever.

John Julius Norwich
Writer and broadcaster

RIDING HIGH

For youngsters going into racing I suggest, 'Stick with the winners because winners never quit and quitters never win.'

Willie Carson
Champion jockey

HOWZAT

My father was a cricket fanatic and actually named me Michael Colin Cowdray so that my initials would be MCC. He started me off at the age of four with a tennis racket and soft ball in our garden. The story goes that while waiting patiently for my father to have a blazer fitted, this horrible precocious little boy said to the tailor, 'When I am in the England team will you make my blazer?'

I was fortunate to have a good eye and to retain my enthusiasm and fitness throughout my career – natural fitness is the most important gift you can be given. In fact, some of the best innings of my life were played in my last season when I was forty-three.

Lord Cowdrey
Cricketer

MOTHER KNOWS BEST?

Ballet is the most demanding of all the performing arts, so to any mothers today with ideas for their daughters, I would give this advice. Don't start them too early: never before three years old – nine or ten is ideal. Make sure the child is well proportioned with small bones and a strong back. Also that she can accept discipline and criticism and much hard work. Most importantly, a successful dancer must have the physical strength and stamina of an ox. If, by good fortune, the child also has grace, talent and personality, who knows, she might do well.

Moira Shearer
Writer and ballerina

DREAMS DO COME TRUE

My dream came true when, aged only fourteen, I was called, at a morning's notice, to take over from Margot Fonteyn. I am a great believer in fate and hard work, for it takes both to make a dream come true; but then, given that break, it took tenacity and spiritual faith to win and retain top position.

Dame Beryl Grey
Prime Ballerina

CHECKLIST FOR SUCCESS

To anyone starting out in journalism I would offer three golden rules. First, it is hard work because the ball is always in your court. Second, a good address book is beyond price. Third, read what others have written and do it better.

Drusilla Beyfus
Journalist

BORN, NOT MADE

Apart from displaying cheek and perseverance, how else can an aspirant recruit to journalism help his cause? I am afraid I have no sure-fire tips, except possibly to stay away from schools of journalism which are worse than useless.

Journalists are born not made. It is a tough old trade. You either have it or you don't and anyone who does have it will be able to think up his own way to get a foot in the door.

Sir Peregrine Worsthorne
Writer and journalist

JUST LUCKY

Sheer luck helped my career as a writer: just saying the right thing at the right time.

Alice Thomas Ellis
Writer

DEDICATED

I always wanted to be a writer; looking back, I think I must have been a rather dull child because I felt so dedicated. But there were so many other things I had to do, as I grew up in wartime, that there was no chance to start novel writing until I was over thirty. Apart from reading the English classics I had no special inspiration. I was influenced early, I think, by the French existentialists, particularly Raymond Queneau and Jean-Paul Sartre.

My first novel *Under the Net* was rather philosophical and I was surprised though of course very pleased by its success. This was a bit of luck, I think, and also a turning point. I also had the advantage of being in love with my future husband, John Bayley, who knows far more about literature than I do and who has always been a great source of ideas and knowledge to me, as well as inspiration.

Dame Iris Murdoch
Author

TELLING A GOOD STORY

To write a successful short story all you really need is about four characters and an incident, such as a man leaving his briefcase on a train and someone running after him, or a disastrous date. It's important to plan a story before you start writing it and to give it a beginning, a middle and an end.

Make the characters into real people. Think of your friends and describe them but make them slightly different. Don't just say 'She had blue eyes and blonde hair', qualify it and say, 'She had Cambridge blue eyes and long blonde hair like an Afghan hound.' Make the characters stand out from the ordinary. Use colours and adjectives as much as you can and keep your sentences short.

Remember that the five senses, how things smell, taste, feel, look and sound – the smoothness of the banisters beneath your hand, the smell of frying bacon drifting up the stairs, the crash of the cat coming through the cat-flap – all bring things to life. As a cumulative effect this makes people know what it is like to be there and makes the whole story much more vivid to the reader.

Why not start by submitting short stories to your local paper or to women's magazines? Keep them to about 3,000 words. Remember to type double spaced and don't have too many lines on a page. If the story looks professional, editors are likely to read it.

Jilly Cooper
Author

DEAR DIARY

Start to keep a diary when you're twenty – or ten is even better: it is never too soon. However callow or ill-written, it will make you a fortune in middle age if you have made a detailed, personal record through your life of the private or personal happenings which have struck you as special. If it is amusing, so much the better. If you can illustrate it with passable sketches, better still. You will later have ready to hand a little piece of history which could develop into a book. Apart from financial possibilities, such a record will enrich the pleasures of memory which fade into a mist without a little restorative help.

Anne Scott-James
Journalist

TAKE IT LYING DOWN

Never dress before lunch. If possible don't even leave your bed (this, however, necessitates a breakfast-bearing slave). Once you are dressed you are in the real world with all its pressing needs and responsibilities – e.g. shopping, cleaning, having cups of coffee with friends. You can do none of this in bed and therefore may, with any luck, be forced to work – to WRITE. Essential activities, such as seeing children off to school, can be achieved if necessary, but always in a dressing-gown. Do not be ashamed of this technique which has been followed by such high achievers as Michael Holroyd and Florence Nightingale. Think of your bed (once day dawns) as a large desk and remember that lap-top computers suit a tray as well as tea and toast.

Lady Rachel Billington
Writer

BY DESIGN

From the age of twelve I knew that I was interested in colour, style, gardens and theatre design, and after conscription in the Army, which taught me discipline, I spent three years at the Central School of Art, where I really learnt how to draw – essential for a designer.

In 1953 my mother bought a house in Belgravia and she let me decorate it exactly as I wanted. This was later photographed by *House & Garden* and suddenly away I went. But it wasn't just good fortune – behind it all was sturdy determination to succeed.

David Hicks
Interior designer

BY DEGREES

The best training for young actors has always been the repertory system – which sadly is no longer in existence.

My advice therefore is to go to university; a degree in any subject you enjoy will give you a qualification to work in other fields should you find yourself temporarily unemployed – most likely these days.

It is not necessary to read drama, unless you wish. You can gain a great deal of practical acting experience by involving yourself in theatre groups and will have the advantage of working (and partying) with students of other disciplines – preferable to spending three years studying with aspirants of one profession only. And finally, don't expect an easy way to success. It's hard work.

Rosalie Crutchley
Actress

GOOD TIMING

Even with talent, it's who you meet at the right
time that tips the scales.

Richard Briers
Actor

HALF AND HALF

Don't even consider becoming an actor unless you
have enormous dedication, tremendous tenacity
and a strong stomach for failure. Don't set out for
life on the boards unless you feel it is something
you just have to do or die.

But I do have important advice on handling one's
income. Right from receiving my first pay packet –
my first regular pay packet anyway – I disciplined
myself to open two bank accounts; one for spending
and one to be nest-egged away for the inevitable
arrival of the little buff envelope from the tax man. I
always put half my earnings into each account. I
have ever since considered that this practice has
enabled me to hold the Inland Revenue at bay all
my working life.

Ian Carmichael
Actor

WINNING BY A NOSE

I prefer not to think that my success as an actor
hangs on my nose, but its shape has certainly
dominated my career.

I was born with a singularly straight and pleasant
nose, which I retained until I was eight, when
Ronnie Williams tripped me up and broke it,
whereafter it was graced with a very large lump.
When I grew up the sinister aspect this gave my face
limited the parts in which I was cast to murderers,

serial killers and the like. Since these parts were in limited supply I decided it was time for a change of face, so to speak, and took myself off to that pioneer of plastic surgery, Sir Archibald MacIndoe, to have the offending lump removed. I suspect the emphasis I placed on it may have coloured his judgment because, when the bandages were removed, what had formerly been convex was now undeniably concave and my nose turned up at the end.

No more murderers – and if it had been changed to the Robert Donat version I longed for I would have been condemned to play straight parts for ever. As it is, the new nose, however unintentional, has given me a certain comedic advantage.

Derek Nimmo
Actor

INSTINCT

Given a job, most actors will work hard. It's having a talent which is peculiarly your own that makes you stand out from the crowd. You have to realize that this originality, this 'you-ness', initially intrigues some and irritates others. Also, one has to follow one's instincts and intuition about which direction to follow and time it right. This instinct is 80 per cent of what success is all about and it's awfully hard to programme.

Maureen Lipman
Actress

BASS INSTINCT

Noel Reddin – bass player with Jimmy Hendrix – said that if you want to go into the music business you should study law and buy a gun.

Nick Mason
Pink Floyd

TRAVELLERS' TALES

In America there are two classes of travel – first class and with children.

Robert Benchley

MORE AND LESS

When travelling, take half the clothes you think you'll need and twice as much money.

Charlotte Lessing
Wine and travel writer

IN POCKET

To save a lot of fumbling in your handbag, wear a coat, dress or jacket with pockets big enough to hold safely your boarding card and credit card (for duty frees) if you are travelling by air, or your ticket and enough change for coffee if you are catching a train.

Jane Fearnley-Whitingstall
Landscape and garden designer

INSIDE OUT

To stop your suit jacket from creasing when you pack it, fold it inside out.

Nigel Amis
Fashion buyer

FIRELIGHTERS

If you are off on a camping safari, take paper knickers. It saves washing and they are good for lighting the fire.

The Lady Cobbold

EN ROUTE

Always take a small roll of Sellotape and some sheets of tinfoil in your hand luggage to seal opened packets of biscuits, wet wipes, etc.

Abha Lessing
Managing director of a computer company

BLACK MARK

Have a black, broad-nibbed felt-tipped pen on you always. It will:

a) hide scuffs on shoes
b) write when your fountain pen runs out
c) act as eye-liner when you are desperate
d) hide holes/ladders in black tights if you use it on your legs. Slovenly but indispensable!

Rabbi Julia Neuberger

A LITTLE KNOWLEDGE

It is fatal, in a foreign country, to give the impression that you speak the language better than you do. For instance, it is no good rehearsing a few telling phrases, such as 'Where is the Post Office?', if you have little hope of understanding the answer. And at more advanced levels, appalling misunderstandings can occur over a dinner table or, worse still, in the doctor's consulting room.

Mrs Alexander Pease

BLIND SPOT

Remember that every car has a blind spot just behind the driver's right shoulder that no rear-view or side mirror can reach. With this in mind, don't pull out to pass without first taking a lightning glance over your shoulder to make sure nothing is lurking there.

Lord Montagu of Beaulieu

ALL DONE WITH MIRRORS

When waiting to overtake, motorcyclists should try never to ride on the rear right-hand corner of a car. The car driver may not be able to see them in the rear-view mirror. It is better to ride directly behind the car so that the rider is visible to the driver but also able to watch the road ahead through the windscreen of the car he is waiting to overtake.

The Lord Strathcarron

WAKEY, WAKEY

I used to have a terrible problem keeping awake when driving long distances. Now I chew sugar-free gum and find it makes all the difference. The only trouble is I hate it, but that's a small price to pay.

The Rt. Hon. John Biffen

RESOLUTION

Make an irrevocable decision never, *ever*, to put anything on the roof of your car. It is inevitable, should you break this resolution, that one day you will forget the handbag, shopping or whatever so placed, and drive away, never to see it again.

Robin Pleydell-Bouverie

HOT AIR

Sometimes in wet weather my car won't start. When this happens I know just what to do. I plug in my wife's hairdryer, put it through the window, open the bonnet and blow hot air on to the electrical leads. In a minute or two we're away.

Tom Cochrane
Plumber

EYES DOWN

One way to avoid being dazzled by the lights of oncoming cars at night is to look downwards along the bonnet and look at the left side of the road.

Garth Colling
Company director

ICE BLOCK

An old blanket makes an excellent ice protector for your windscreen and doesn't seem to suffer from build-up of ice as card or plastic do. Remember, however, not to leave a soggy blanket in the boot of your car.

Jo Cornley
Director of Administration and Finance,
Katharine House Hospice

LOOK AHEAD

Driving along a busy motorway, try to keep an eye on the car three or four ahead, watching for its braking lights. If you look only at the vehicle immediately in front of you, you will not see the braking lights further ahead, which will alert you to an emergency.

Lord Montagu of Beaulieu

PASTE IT

When your car windscreen is smeared and oily, wash it with toothpaste and water. When it is thoroughly rinsed you'll find it fabulously clear.

Nigel Havers
Actor

KEEP COOL

If you want to keep cool in your car in hot weather, buy a white one. Whereas dark colours absorb heat, white repels it; therefore a white car will be several degrees cooler than a dark one. On the next sunny day walk down a line of parked cars, putting your hand on each as you pass. You will be amazed at the difference in temperatures.

Mrs Gerhard Bulle

ONE FOR THE ROAD

The best way to arrive cool, calm and collected after a tiring drive is to take plenty of talking books with you. Though not as satisfying as the written word, most of them are beautifully read and it's a particularly good way of catching up on all the classics you would probably never get round to otherwise.

Rose Pelly
Secretary

SPARE TIME

Don't waste time when you're sitting on the loo or in the car. Have something to study. That's how I passed the Staff College exams when working under somewhat trying conditions.

Field Marshal Sir Nigel Bagnall

BE PREPARED

Unexpected delays and breakdowns not only can but frequently do happen, so when visiting people you don't know well it's wise to make sure you have their telephone number as well as their address with you.

Mrs Hugh Rance

WORTH REPEATING

Everyone knows this but it is worth saying again: drink nothing but water and don't eat anything at all if you want to avoid jet lag and arrive fresh at the end of a long flight.

Mrs John Falloon

HIGH AND DRY

Long-haul flights are known to be exceedingly de-hydrating and make one's skin dry and flaky. As well as drinking lots of water, get an aerosol Evian spray and squirt your face at regular intervals.

Mrs Jeffrey Julian

STRETCH OUT

Travelling in an aeroplane, wear clothes which are as much like pyjamas as your sense of style and the formality of your meeting-party will allow. Stretch fabrics are fine but make sure there is a lot of cotton in them. Alternatively I've seen business-men who have changed back again into a smart suit after a long flight spent in a track suit. So sensible.

Sir Anthony Kenny
Warden of Rhodes College

LOOSEN UP

When I go on a long-haul flight I change into a kaftan. Like undressing on the beach, I can take most of my clothes off underneath it – and put them on again – which means I don't necessarily have to queue for the loo. And of course, I am very comfortable in such a loose-fitting garment.

Mrs Annie Howard

KNEES UP

Always carry a small rigid suitcase (or beauty case) as cabin baggage on a plane to use as a footstool. It vastly improves the balance of your body weight in the in-flight sitting position – and minimizes swollen ankles.

Anne Gregg
Journalist and broadcaster

SAFETY SNACK

I have a friend who always takes hard-boiled eggs with her when travelling in inhospitable countries, thus ensuring that, for the first week at least, she has a hygienically wrapped, bug-free snack.

Mrs Francis Sitwell

SNEAK A SNACK

The perfect picnic lunch can be made from breakfast left-overs – ideal when staying bed-and-breakfast in a hotel. Slice down the middle of a piece of toast, between the two toasted sides (so that it opens out into two thin pieces) and spread one side lightly with mustard, the other with marmalade, and put the two together with bacon in the middle. Delicious later and, what's more, it's free.

Richard Birch Reynardson

TOWEL DRY

An old friend of my stepmother's who did a lot of travelling advised me many moons ago that if one wants one's undies to dry overnight at a hotel, after washing one should towel them dry as much as possible. I wrap mine in a bath towel and stand on it before hanging them up. That way they will certainly be dry in the morning.

Mrs Miguel Ferrer

THE BEST ROOM

Here's a way to be sure of a good hotel room when you have booked in on a package tour. Take the trouble to write to the hotel, explaining that you are arriving on such-and-such a date with whatever tour operator and would like to have the best available accommodation. If you are bringing children, ask if you can have adjoining rooms. You might add that you have heard how good the hotel is and that you are much looking forward to your stay with them. On arrival, mention your name to the receptionist and you should be greeted with open arms.

David Hornick
Hire-car chauffeur

SLEEP WELL

When you are staying in a twin-bedded hotel room and want to be sure of a good night's sleep, always choose the bed furthest away from the telephone. The mattress of the other bed will have been ruined by hundreds of fat-bummed businessmen who have sat on the edge, talking on the telephone.

The Earl of Portarlington

SAY THANK YOU

If, after a holiday, you have particularly enjoyed a stay in a hotel or rented apartment, and especially if you would like to return, it is a good idea to write to the owners and tell them they have done a good job. Too often the only letters they get are ones of complaint, so they will remember you with affection and put themselves out to give you a good room and best attention next time.

Janet Ferrer
Hotel proprietor

FIRE, FIRE

Fires do occur in hotels and it is as well to think about what to do if the alarm goes off. When you arrive, check where the nearest exits are. In an emergency, make sure you grab your room key so that you can get back in – perhaps it was a false alarm or maybe the smoke is so thick you have to dash back to get a wet towel to wrap around your face.

Edmund Rothschild
Banker

QUICK THINKING

Should the fire alarm sound when you are staying in a hotel, snatch a blanket off the bed to keep you warm if you have to stand around outside for long.

Mrs Richard Malone

FORWARD PLANNING

Be very generous when you tip the person who carries your luggage to your hotel room. He will tell the rest of the staff of your largesse and you will get excellent service.

The Lord Birdwood

TIP TOP

Give large tips at a restaurant you might want to go back to. It is the little bit that you don't *have* to give that secures goodwill.

The Lord Quinton

HEAR, HEAR

Instead of a camera, next time you go on holiday take a cassette tape recorder. Sound conjures up pictures in the mind that bring back far more vivid memories than photographs.

John Whitney
Former Director General, IBA

ON THE RECORD

Videoed events, if precious, should be re-recorded on to professional quality videotape, or they will fade over ten years or so. Expensive perhaps, but worth it.

Dr Neil Hunter

OLD FRIEND

When you get too old for soldiering or mountaineering or camping out, do not give away your good old sleeping bag. Keep it as part of your luggage. There is no cold like the cold of other people's houses.

The Rt. Hon. Sir James Ramsden

BACK TO FRONT

Visiting a popular exhibition or art gallery, start at the end and go backwards – the crowds are always at the beginning.

Dr Alan Borg
Director, Victoria & Albert Museum

ART APPRECIATION

When I was a child my mother would take me to the National Gallery, Tate Gallery, etc. and allow me to look at only one picture. As a result I really remembered that one and longed to dwell on others that I was hurried past, giving me a lasting pleasure in and curiosity for looking at paintings.

Lord Linley
Furniture designer

TAKE A VIEW

If you are tall, take binoculars to a crowded art gallery, so that you can get a good view over people's heads. If you're short you can probably worm your way to the front anyway.

Jane Hudson
Entrepreneur

MISS A MEAL

Avoid the crowds when visiting popular exhibitions in France by going at lunchtime on Sunday, but check first to make sure they aren't closed.

James Brockman
Bookbinder

LATE ARRIVALS

Taking visitors to very popular and busy tourist attractions such as Madame Tussaud's or the Tower of London, plan to arrive an hour or so before closing time. The hordes will be leaving and you will have a clear tour round.

Lady Owen

CLOSE UP

Architecture is one of my great interests and whenever I go sightseeing I make sure I have my binoculars with me so that I can look at the details of a building. Gargoyles on church towers, delicate stonework, pillars and statues that are too far away to be appreciated by the naked eye can all be seen and studied.

Mrs Michael Heseltine

JUST IN CASE

Every time I pass a church
I pay a little visit,
So when at last I'm carried in
The Lord won't say, 'Who is it?'

Spotted by Angela Pelly in a village church

PERSONAL
APPEARANCES

The same costume will be:

Daring	...	*a year before its time*
Smart	...	*in its time*
Dowdy	...	*a year after its time*
Hideous	...	*10 years after its time*
Ridiculous	...	*20 years after its time*
Amusing	...	*30 years after its time*
Quaint	...	*50 years after its time*
Charming	...	*70 years after its time*
Romantic	...	*100 years after its time*
Beautiful	...	*150 years after its time*

JAMES LAVER, FASHION WRITER

NO-PRESS APPROACH

When you unpack a suitcase, or take off crumpled clothes, to remove the creases hang them up and spray them with a fine cloud of cold water from one of those cheap plastic atomizer sprays you can find at garden centres. Spray velvets on the inside, not the outside.

Min Hogg
Editor, Interiors

LESS IS MORE

Nothing to wear? Chuck out instead of buying in. Edit a wardrobe full of tat and you'll find at least two things that will look terrific with your one good pair of trousers.

Shirley Lowe
Writer

MORE DASH THAN CASH

These days you need a vast clothes allowance to dress in each season's new colours – and to hang on to them too long risks such unflattering remarks as 'Oh, God, she's wearing her purple again!' Far better, especially if you're getting on a bit and strong colours are less than kind, is to stick to the basic colours – the navies, blacks, browns and greys in all their infinite variety – and add the fashionable colours in small doses. Things like the 'right' colour shirt, sweater, scarf or jacket prove you're no frump, but don't cost the earth and will be much welcomed by one of the many charity shops afterwards.

Sylvia Lamond
Writer

ON THE LEVEL

To level or shorten a skirt when you have no one to mark it for you, stretch a piece of string between two chairs at the height required and rub chalk on the string. Put your skirt on and turn slowly, touching the string all the way round. The hem will then be marked at the perfect height.

Roland Klein
Fashion designer

SAY CHEESE

If you are one of the many who regards having their photograph taken as a form of Chinese torture, these three steps should help. One, relax your body by shrugging your shoulders and shaking your hands – both release tension and help to avoid the startled-rabbit look. Two, turn your shoulders slightly so that you're not sitting square on to the camera – the least flattering position. Three, before the shutter clicks, look just above the camera lens.

Linda Burns
Beauty editor, Scene

GREAT MINDS

I firmly believe in Oscar Wilde's famous quip that 'There is only one thing in the world worse than being talked about, and that is not being talked about.' My own humble adage – 'It's better to be looked over than over-looked' – is hardly in the same class, but has certainly helped me laugh off many an awkward moment.

Mrs Howard Bannister

HALF SHOD

If you are a man, when you are in Italy, buy shoes. The equivalent article is only half – or maybe a third – of the price it is here in England. (I do not know if this applies to women's shoes.)

The Lord Quinton

FEET FIRST

I've never forgotten my father's advice, which was that you can always tell a gentleman by his shoes.

Mrs Jeffrey Peate

DON'T BE SNIFFY

If you've got really whiffy sneakers, shake in some deodorized cat-litter and leave overnight.

Mrs Peter Tayler

FOOTNOTE

Here is a piece of advice for any man invited to a traditional dinner in Japan: make sure your socks are immaculate, as you are likely to have to take your shoes off before you sit down to dine.

The Rt. Hon. Lord Lawson

HAT TRICK

If the artificial flowers on that gorgeous hat you packed away last summer are looking limp and jaded, get hold of some hair-tongs. As long as you don't overheat them, they are marvellous for smoothing down leaves and curling petals.

Hélène de Reboul
Hatmaker

IN THE CREASE

Creases in trousers can be sharpened by rubbing a piece of dry soap along the crease on the wrong side of the fabric.

Roland Klein
Fashion designer

A QUESTION OF CONFIDENCE

If you lack confidence going into designer shops take a bodyguard in the shape of a good, strong friend. You'll have a great time and no one will intimidate you into buying anything you don't really want.

David Shilling
Hat designer

SIT IN IT

Of course you take a good look at your back view when you are trying on a dress in a shop, but it is worth remembering to sit down in it as well. Split skirts can gape open in an unnervingly revealing way, and anything too tight can spell disaster.

Mrs Michael Devas

IN PRINT

Newspaper, worn under your clothes rather than expensive underwear, will keep you warm in very cold winds. It has the advantage of being cheap and easy to remove – as tramps and motorcyclists have known for years. A word of caution, however. Use only good quality broadsheet newspapers as the print of the tabloids can come off on clothing.

The Lord Falkland

COLD COMFORT

Instant cooler for hot days: always keep a spare pair of knickers in the fridge.

Anne Gregg
Journalist and broadcaster

IN THE HOT SEAT

Keeping dry when ski-ing in extreme conditions is vital. A soaking wet hat is bad enough – but a bare head is dangerous. So tuck a second 'emergency' hat into the crotch of your pants when dressing. It does not take up a precious pocket, and it stays dry and warm for when you need it.

Ueli Frei
Swiss mountain guide

PARCHED

In very dry weather one can have problems with static electricity. If you've run out of anti-static spray use a fine-mist water-sprayer (the sort used for spraying the leaves of indoor plants) on slips and petticoats that cling. I also find that a dry climate affects the elasticity in tights and stockings, so that they ladder easily. Keeping them in the freezer will overcome this problem – but remember to take them out the night before you want to wear them.

Lady Appleyard

THE PERFECT DISGUISE

My way of disguising small holes, burns or stains on delicate fabrics like blouses, slips, bras, pillowcases and so on, is to embroider a simple motif – flowers are easiest – over or around the mark. If you use thread that is the same colour as the fabric, the design will blend in and almost disappear. If you choose a contrasting colour – repeating the motif elsewhere if necessary to balance up – it will look as if you actually meant it to be there!

Maria Montes-Riveiro
Seamstress

HERE'S THE SNAG

When you've snagged your sweater and pulled a stitch loose, try this way of putting it neatly back in its place. Push a needle threaded with cotton through the sweater from back to front in the exact spot where the loose stitch is. Loop the cotton round the aforesaid loose stitch and then simply push the needle back to the underside of the garment again. The offending snag will pull through with it.

Mrs Howard Bannister

ON YOUR MARKS

Getting marks off cloth can be a hazardous business, frequently creating new marks in place of the old. If the damage is fairly minor, try the dressmaker's trick of rubbing like fabric with like – silk with silk, suede with suede, etc.

Mrs Allen Muschamp

OFF WITH THE LEGS

Cut the legs off laddered tights and you are left with a well-fitted pair of pants to wear underneath tickly woolly tights. The edges don't even fray.

June Zetter
Housekeeper

THINK THIN

If you want to look slim, loosen your belt. Although squeezing into a smaller size makes one feel thinner, in fact the effect is to make one look fatter. Sad but true.

William Gronow Davies
Artist

LITTLE AND LEAN

Dress lean. Only Kate Moss can layer amusing little woollen garments on top of each other without resembling an overweight Eskimo. And it's generally accepted that the cleverest make-up looks as though you're wearing none at all.

Shirley Lowe
Writer

UNDERCOVER

Keep scented soap loose among your underclothes.

Soap lasts longer if it is kept for a while before it is used, and your nighties and things will smell wonderful.

Lady Georgina Coleridge
Journalist and author

WEAR IT WITH PRIDE

Gloria Swanson said of Cecil B. de Mille that he wore his baldness like an expensive hat, as though it were out of the question for him to have hair like other men. It helps to make any deficiencies part of one's charm.

Garry O'Connor
Author and biographer

GOOD HAIR DAY

When you wash your hair, brush the lather through with your hairbrush and comb. It's good for the hair and gets the brush and comb clean at the same time. Of course, they have to be rinsed as well but that can also be done at the same time as your hair.

Prunella Scales
Actress

BACK TO THE ROOTS

To give longer, finer hair more volume and 'body', bend down and brush it firmly forwards from the nape to the crown. Then spray the roots with firm-hold hairspray before sitting up and shaking the hair down again, smoothing and shaping it with your fingers.

Douglas von Katzer
Hairstylist

TAKE A SHINE

Before the days of a million choices of shampoos and conditioners our mothers gave their hair a last rinse in vinegar and water. It is still hard to beat for really shiny hair and very inexpensive.

Countess Bathurst

STATIC CONTROL

When you've just washed your hair and can't do a thing with it, when it's all 'fly away' and full of static electricity, you will find that a styling gel is much more effective than a mousse.

Nicky Betteridge
Hairstylist

EMERGENCY MEASURE

If you dye your hair to hide the grey, you will know that just before you can get to the hairdresser a grown-out edge of white will appear at your hairline. If you're going somewhere special, in the emergency, brush the tell-tale line with mascara.

Kathy O'Shea
Hairstylist

INDIRECTLY

For a smoother-looking hairstyle, don't use your hairspray direct – spray it on to the brush instead.

Douglas von Katzer
Hairstylist

HALF AND HALF

Skin that's going through a particularly dry patch will welcome – and respond to – massage with a

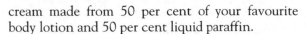

cream made from 50 per cent of your favourite body lotion and 50 per cent liquid paraffin.

Linda Burns
Beauty Editor, Scene

SOFTENING-UP PROCESS

To keep your make-up brushes in perfect condition, soften them up after washing with a dab of conditioner (they are made of hair, after all) before the final rinse. A similar approach works for velour powder puffs, too, except in their case the softener should be a fabric one.

Emma Kotch
Make-up artist

FACELIFT

An unforgiving nature reflects in the face. Holding negative energy drags down the facial muscles, puckers one's frown and causes lines around the mouth. Working daily on forgiveness (forgiving oneself as well as one's enemies) is the cheapest, most effective facelift in the whole wide world. All it requires is love and discipline.

Sarah Miles
Actress

LOOK AGAIN

Every ten years or so one should re-assess one's appearance. A hairstyle that looked great when you were younger may look dated and not so flattering to an even slightly-older face.

Jane Tyler
Make-up artist

FACING UP TO THE WORST

I believe in knowing the worst, and on the assumption that others can probably see me better than I can see myself, I always make up my face looking into the strongest magnifying mirror I can find. A depressing experience every time but at least I'm not fooling myself.

The Lady Wardington

CHEEKY

Don't bother to buy rouge. Mix a little of your lipstick on fingertips with a scrap of your foundation cream, then dab it lightly on your cheeks and smooth in. This has the advantage of exactly toning with your lips.

Linda Tulley
Make-up artist

ALL SET

To avoid the over-powdered look that can be so ageing, spray your face very lightly all over with Evian water after you've finished making up. This also 'sets' make-up and helps it to last longer.

Emma Kotch
Make-up artist

NAILING THE PROBLEM

Nail varnish will last longer and clog less if you keep it in the fridge.

Christine Goodwill
Office manager

THE ACID TEST

Pearls react to the acid in skin and while they will

remain gleaming and translucent on one person for a lifetime, a change of wearer can 'kill' them, turning them dull and pot-like. It can be asking for disappointment to buy a second-hand string that may have been worn by someone whose skin is not compatible with yours. My advice is always to buy new ones.

John Lloyd Morgan
Jeweller

FACE FLATTERY

When you're not as young as you were, it's wiser to avoid elaborate earrings, especially drop ones and big 'dome' shapes. Small is infinitely more flattering to faces that (perish the thought) have started to sag.

Laurie Purden
Journalist

IN THE PINK

Women over fifty should always have at least one pink shirt in their wardrobe. It's much cheaper than a facelift.

Anne Dickinson
Company director

HEALTH AND RELAXATION

A thing of beauty is a joy for ever: …
A bower quiet for us and a sleep
Full of sweet dreams, and health, and
quiet breathing.

JOHN KEATS

BE GOOD

Should you suffer a heart attack, start obeying your wife, even if you have never done so before.

The Lady Somerleyton

IDEAL REGIME

For perfect health, start the day with a small glass (two tablespoons) of aloe vera juice, followed by a mug of hot water – add the juice of half an orange or lemon if you like. Till lunchtime, eat only fruit or drink fruit juice (cranberry is good mixed with orange juice). For lunch in warm weather eat a salad and in the winter have vegetable soup. Eat a normal cooked meal in the evening, composed of

152

cooked vegetables with pasta or grains for the most part, with oily fish or chicken maybe twice a week and meat and eggs once each. Take exercise three to four times a week – forty minutes' brisk walking or twenty minutes' swimming – plus a brisk daily walk round a few blocks.

This is an ideal to which I aspire but don't always succeed. I can't resist a cup of coffee mid-morning and a glass of vodka or wine most evenings.

Arabella Boxer
Cookery writer

LUBRICATE THE SYSTEM

My recipe for keeping the system working well is to drink a glass of hot water mixed with the juice of half a lemon last thing at night, and repeat the dose first thing in the morning.

Ruth Brass
Schoolteacher

THE CHINESE ART OF PRESERVING HEALTH

The following is from an early eighteenth-century commonplace book given to me when I was twenty by someone who obviously thought I needed it.

Breakfast betimes: it is not good to go out fasting. In winter a glass or two of good wine is an excellent preservation against unwholesome air.

Make a hearty meal about noon; eat plain meats only; avoid salted meats – those who eat them much have pale faces, a slow pulse and are full of corrupt humours.

Sup betimes – let your meats be neither too much nor too little done.

Sleep not until two hours within eating; begin your meal with a little tea and wash your mouth with it afterwards.

I do indeed drink wine, but never more than four or five glasses.

Immediately after you awake, rub your breast where your heart lies with the palm of your hand; and avoid a stream of wind as you would an arrow.

On coming out of a hot bath or after hard labour do not expose your body to cold. It is unwholesome to fan yourself during perspiration.

Philip Astley-Jones
Furniture restorer

SLIM-LINE LARDER

My first step towards cooperating with my husband's slimming diet was to sort out the larder, keeping only suitable ingredients. I found it much easier to stick to Nigel's criteria when faced in my store only with ingredients that were permissible, in much the same way that a ruthless wardrobe sort-out limits the agony of choice every morning of what top to wear with which bottom.

The Lady Lawson

CRAMP CURE

Always have a bottle of water and salt solution beside your bed to cure a sudden attack of cramp.

Maximillian van Hoot
Art dealer

PULL THE PLUG

There have been many cases of drowning even in a

few inches of bathwater, so never stand up in the bath without pulling the plug out. Were you to slip, bang your head into unconsciousness and slip back into the water it would be a soapy end.

The Lord Hanson
Chairman, Hanson Trust

THE VOICE OF EXPERIENCE

With twenty-five years' experience of life in a wheelchair, these hints might be helpful to others in a like position, or their families.

Choice of self-propelled wheelchair to be as light as possible – preferably under 30 lb/13.5 kg – for the sake of relatives who have to load it into cars.

Wheelchair main wheels to be no bigger than 20 in/50 cm diameter for ease of transfer to baths, loos, beds, cars, etc. This size of wheel allows a more natural movement of arms and shoulders than larger wheels and, at the same time, aids manoeuvrability.

The wheelchair should have a shelf under it for carrying documents, cameras, books (or in my case as many as six bottles).

A lap table consisting of a simple leather case – artificial leather suffices – with a zip compartment, inside which is a firm board cut to size to provide rigidity. This rests on the thighs within the span of the armrests. It is essential for writing and can also be used for eating or drinking if necessary.

Inexpensive gloves as provided to forestry workers not only keep hands clean when handling the wheels (after all, people usually avoid rubbing their hands on the soles of their shoes) but give non-slip grip, useful for handling wheel rims and getting into a car.

The Duke of Buccleuch

MULTIPLE VISION

If you need to wear spectacles for reading and can never find them when you want them, don't worry about buying lots of expensive prescription glasses from the optician. Go out to the local chemist and supplement your good pair with half a dozen that suit your sight, and spread them around the house.

Patrick Trevor-Roper
Ophthalmic surgeon

COLD START

I have used this cold preventative for years and it nearly always works. At the first sign of that ominous scrapey feeling at the back of the throat, take a 0.035 oz/1000mg non-fizzy vitamin C tablet with a glass of milk. Breathe steam for as long as you can bear it (forty-five minutes is recommended). Get as much rest as you can and avoid sugar, alcohol, cold cures, smoking and smoky atmospheres. Repeat this preventative if you feel yourself succumbing.

Lady Kenny

LISTINGS

Before visiting a busy GP, jot down all the things you want to talk to him or her about. If you don't, you can be sure you'll find yourself standing outside the surgery with a vital question left unasked.

Laurie Purden
Journalist

TAKE A FRIEND

When you are very worried about your health, take a friend with you when you go to see your doctor.

He – or she – will be able to listen less emotionally and remember better what has been said, and you will be able to discuss the diagnosis rationally later. So often one comes away from the practitioner with only a vague idea of what the GP has told you. Of course, you could take a tape recorder but this might inhibit the doctor.

The Lord Cullen

DRIED OUT

Fitness is essential for me – I cycle at least 62 miles/100 km a day to keep in training – and I enjoy a drink with friends. But I never have anything to drink, not even water, with meals because I believe it dilutes the digestive juices.

Abraham Olano
World cycling champion

IN THE BAG

If you suffer from claustrophobia or panic attacks, always carry a brown paper bag. Then, if you have an attack, just breathe deeply and slowly into the bag until your respiration becomes normal again.

Kevin Scott
Auxiliary nurse

COMPARISONS

To avoid feeling fat, mix with people bigger than you are. To avoid whingeing about your advanced age, mix with people who are older. Do not, however, mix with people who are less intelligent, because although it makes you feel clever, it's hard work and boring.

Lynne Truss
Writer and novelist

MYRTLE FOR MIDGES

During a recent photographic session on a boggy river bank we were beset with midges. A kindly fisherman came running to us, bearing bunches of myrtle. On his suggestion we rubbed the green leaves on all our exposed skin and at the end of the day were delighted to find not a bite in sight.

Susan George
Actress

KITCHEN CURES

Should you cut yourself in the kitchen, two remedies will be instantly to hand. Ground cinnamon sprinkled on the wound will stop the bleeding, and the white of egg will protect it from bacterial infection.

June Zetter
Housekeeper

ON THE TIP OF THE TONGUE

Fits of sneezing – such a trial at inconvenient moments – can often be stopped by curling the tip of your tongue upwards and pressing it firmly against the roof of your mouth.

Mrs Garth Colling

AT A PINCH

If you have a nose bleed, forget ancient remedies such as cold keys down your back. Sit still and pinch the fleshy part of your nose for five minutes.

The Hon. W. S. Pease

A STITCH IN TIME

When you get a 'stitch' in your side, bend your

knees to touch your chin. Three times should be enough.

Charlotte Colling
Student

BRAINY

I read somewhere that exercising the brain is just as important a part of keeping fit as exercising the body: doing a crossword every day, reciting the alphabet backwards, learning a new fact or one verse of a new-to-you poem. I don't know if it works but it sounds eminently sensible and I'm certainly going to try it.

Laurie Purden
Journalist

WHEN LEFT IS RIGHT

As a high proportion of the population are right-handed, when taking your coffee break in a café where you are doubtful about the washing-up, hold the cup in your left hand and drink out of the other, unsullied, side.

Douglas von Katzer
Hairstylist

A NEW ANGLE

The hygienist at my dentist's is always very in-sistent that I use floss and brush my teeth well every day. Nothing new there, but I think I have found a new route to really thorough cleaning. I am right-handed, but two or three times a week I brush my teeth with my left hand, thus getting quite a different angle with the bristles.

Obbie Waller
Interior decorator

STEADY GAZE

My certain cure for hiccups – everyone has one – is to persuade the sufferer to gaze unblinking into my also unblinking eyes for as long as it takes. This works best with people you don't know very well.

The Lady Wardington

TIE FOR A STY

In Russia they say that a sty in the eye can be cured by tying a thread of cotton round your little finger, just tightly enough for you to feel it.

Charlotte Hobson
Slavist

SETTLER

An upset stomach can be quickly settled by drinking a glass of soda water laced with a few drops of Angostura Bitters.

Angus Forsyth
Lloyds underwriter

CATNAP

If you begin to feel tired and try to fight it, listen to your sensible self and catnap. Then you will return to your tasks with renewed vigour.

The Countess of Minto

TUNE IN

If you are a poor sleeper and determined not to take sleeping pills, turn your radio on as soon as you wake in the night. The World Service takes over from BBC Radio 4 LW and the voices of the newsreaders and commentators are wonderfully soothing.

The Lady Carrington

AWAY, DULL CARE

Put your cares away with your garments when you go to bed, so that you may sleep better, and resume them in the morning.

The Marchioness of Salisbury

NIGHT RHYMES

Try reciting poetry to yourself in order to get to sleep. It's very soporific, but you might have to do some preliminary homework!

Field Marshal Sir Nigel Bagnall

SWEET DREAMS

It is often possible to get back to sleep quickly if you try to remember the dream that woke you up.

William Gronow-Davis
Artist

THE ABC OF SLEEP

When you are having one of those nights when you just can't get to sleep, play the Alphabet Game. You rarely finish it. Choose a subject – composers, car models, cities, friends – and name them alphabetically. It works for children too, specially with simple subjects such as animals: anteater, baboon, cat, dog, etc.

The Lady Chichester

DOUBLE UP

If you find a double duvet a bit overwhelming, try two single ones on a double bed. This also allows for variable thickness of covering.

Mrs Teddy Hall

PEACE AT LAST

To stop your partner snoring, shout 'STOP SNORING'. Amazingly this never seems to wake them and usually works. If not, gently pinch the offending nose until the automatic reaction of a snuffled shake of the head moves their position without properly awakening them and snoring stops.

Mrs M. Bridges

SPEND

Never economize on your shoes or your bed, because if you're not in one you're in the other.

The Countess Cathcart

INSTANT WAKEFULNESS

When the alarm goes in the morning and I just *can't* wake up, I find that if I twiddle my fingers and thumbs I can spring out of bed immediately – well, almost.

Charlotte Hobson
Slavist

PERFECT PEACE

A little sit-down after lunch is a treat I indulge in more and more nowadays and I frequently find it develops into a snooze or even a deep sleep. But in case I should sleep too long I put the kitchen timer beside me and set it for an hour – or whatever length of time I can spare. It gives me great peace of mind and a good rest.

Mrs Michael Rooney

FEET UP

Lying down for five or ten minutes each day with

one's head lower than one's feet not only induces a feeling of well-being but, so they say, retards baldness and grey hair.

Mrs Lawrie Meredith-Owens

WAKE UP

Sleepwalking can be prevented by putting a large wet cloth on the floor by the side of the bed. As soon as the somnambulist's bare feet touch the cloth he or she will wake up.

Lady Waterlow

A GOOD SOAK

When you are completely exhausted and short of time, five to ten minutes lying in a hot bath is more renewing and refreshing than the same amount of time lying on the bed.

The Rt. Hon. John Biffen

DON'T FORGET

If there are important things I particularly want to remember the next day, just before I go to sleep I run through them in my mind and commit the noun of the errand or job to be done to memory, and then the first letter. For instance, buy Stamps, pick up Tickets, take dog to Vet. I go to sleep thinking S,T,V, and in the morning the nouns and the tasks they represent return in a flash.

The Viscountess Eccles

TWO FOR ONE

Go fly fishing. You come home with the world and supper sorted out.

Jonathan Powell
Director of drama, Carlton Television

LESS STRESS

Stress management is a term which seems, of late, to have crept into our vocabulary. I have tried a variety of methods of relaxing and at the top of my list is daily t'ai chi. However, this requires an excellent teacher, uninterrupted time and many years' practice to perfect. More readily to hand is my computer bridge machine, which ensures total diversion from any knotty problem. Concentrating on an instant rubber of bridge refocuses the mind and the problem is either solved or minimized.

The Lady Ashcombe

JUGGLING WITH JIGSAWS

As a family, we find great relaxation in jigsaws, but we don't like them to be too easy. We always turn the pieces out on to the lid, so that we can't see the picture, and we make a rule to start in the middle and do the outside last. When we want to make things *really* tricky, we mix a couple of old jigsaws together.

Alderman Sir Brian Jenkins
Former Lord Mayor of London

WALK AWAY

About a year ago, when my life seemed beset with problems, I took to taking a really long walk by myself in the countryside at least once a week. The exercise and the fresh air cleared my mind, giving me space to think clearly, and most of my worries evaporated.

Tony Hilton
Alarm engineer

TROUBLED TIMES

*It's over and it can't be helped, and that's one
consolation as they always say in Turkey, ven they
cuts the wrong man's head off.*

Charles Dickens

BREAKING THE NEWS

It is better to tell someone bad news in the
morning after they have slept, rather than last
thing at night or during the night. It might not
always be possible but it is a good guideline.

Hugo Vickers
Biographer

LOOKING BACK

When life is proving particularly difficult or you
are going through an unhappy time, console
yourself with the knowledge that it will almost
undoubtedly turn out to be a time of learning and
development when viewed retrospectively.

Lady Weldon

BRIDGING THE GAP

I have found this idea, written by Arthur Koestler, enormously valuable. He believes that ordinary mortal life is played out in two stages, situated on two different levels. Let us call them the trivial plane and the tragic plane. On some rare occasions, when confronted with death or engulfed in the oceanic feeling, we seem to fall through the stage trap and are transferred to the tragic or absolute plane.

Then all at once the pursuits of our daily routine appear as shallow, trifling vanities. But once safely back on the trivial plane we dismiss the experiences of the other as phantasms of overstrung nerves.

The highest form of human creativity is the endeavour to bridge the gap between the two planes.

Jeremy Irons
Actor

TAKE YOUR TIME

'Cool it' and 'Sleep on it' are refrains that jingle in one's mind when anger and irritation strike. How much more important this is in times of acute stress, such as when a marriage breaks up. Give yourself time to come out of shock and get back to a more normal frame of mind before deciding anything. It may take six months or longer.

Professional and family advice is no substitute for making up your own mind. Do not allow others to bulldoze you into vital decisions such as selling your home or changing jobs. Don't forget that even the most well-meaning like to tidy you away, and even though you evoke pity and concern there is an element of exasperation as consciences are pricked.

The deeper the blow the longer it takes to get

back to normal. Even more important, remember 'Laugh and the world laughs with you, weep and you weep alone.'

Countess Michalowski

SOOTHING

A wise friend advised me when my life seemed very difficult and I was depressed, each day to:

a) do something for someone else.
b) do something for myself.
c) take ten minutes every day to pray, or meditate or just sit quietly and clear my mind of troubles and think of something I liked to think about.

Eileen Atkins
Actress

LITTLE THINGS

After any major sadness or crisis in life, make a conscious effort to recapture joy in very small things: be it the first snowdrop, dew on a spider's web, the song of a bird, the sun on your back – or even something as simple as feeling just the right temperature at a particular moment. But it takes practice.

Mary Sheepshanks
Author

BALANCING ACT

Even a happy life cannot be without a measure of darkness and the word 'happiness' would lose its meaning if it were not balanced by sadness.

Rula Lenska
Actress

UPS AND DOWNS

I would say this of sadness: without it, what price is happiness? A man who knows no valley can never find a hilltop.

The Lord McAlpine of West Green

IN THE MIND

Let us be of good cheer by remembering that the misfortunes that are hardest to bear are those that never come.

The Earl Kitchener of Khartoum
quoting James Russell Lowell

ACCEPTANCE

Don't worry too much about the future. True peace of mind can come only if, having done one's best, one can then accept without question whatever is to come.

Mr and Mrs David Hodges

INSURANCE

Think of the worst that could happen, plan for it, and then forget all about it.

Mary, Countess of Strathmore

DON'T WORRY

There are only two things to worry about. You are either sick or you are well. If you are well you have nothing to worry about. If you are sick you have two things to worry about. Either you get well or you will die. If you get well there is nothing to worry about. If you die there are two things to worry about. Either you will go to Heaven or Hell. If you go to Heaven you have nothing to worry about. If you go to Hell you will be so busy shaking hands with all your friends, you won't have time to worry.

Mrs Richard Malone

WRITE IT OFF

It is marvellous how many worries dissolve when you write them down on a piece of paper and then review the likelihood of their eventualizing. Nine times out of ten that likelihood will be remote.

Paul Wilson
Author

COME OUTSIDE

When you feel a row coming on, and the words 'we have to talk' spoken in a certain tone are heard, grab the dogs' leads and head outside. Outdoors, far away from tempting items of household china, an argument can follow its natural, expressive course. Instead of being confined to hissed whispers (to avoid alarming the children) feelings can be bellowed to the four winds – the dogs don't mind a bit and generally join in with joyful barking.

Hugh Palmer
Location photographer

DIG IT

If you are fed up with everyone around you, find a large patch of ground elder or bindweed and dig away at the longest roots you can find. So satisfying, since your activity will clear both your mind and the ground.

Mrs John Hayward

WATCH YOUR WORDS

Be very careful about what you say when you are in the room with someone who appears to be in a coma, perhaps a stroke victim. Although they cannot respond they may be able to hear and understand every word spoken.

Martin May-Smith

IN TOUCH

Try not to avoid someone who is recently bereaved, even if you are not sure what to say. A handshake, a smile or a hug, depending on how well you know them, will show that person that you care and they will feel less isolated.

Dr Clare Terrell

JUST LISTEN

When a friend needs consoling, do not give in to the temptation of telling stories similar to theirs of disaster or bereavement. It is something people often do to show empathy but nothing is more tiresome than other people's problems when you want to focus on your own. Listening is by far the best form of consolation.

Giles Andreae
Cartoonist and children's author

FOOD FIRST

On hearing of the death of a close friend, go round with a box of delicious food and strong drink. The family will have forgotten the shopping and will be distraught.

Jennifer Paterson
Food writer and TV personality

LOOK ON THE BRIGHT SIDE

Writing a letter of sympathy, focus on what you enjoyed about your friendship with the deceased. His wit made you laugh perhaps, or he was generous with his best claret. She inspired you to attempt something worthwhile, and brought joy to those around her. Dwelling on death brings no comfort.

Sir Martin Jacomb
Chairman, The British Council

DUG OUT

I was distraught after my father died but found great consolation in weeding and digging in the garden. I strongly recommend this therapy in times of grief.

The Lord Wardington

PAUSE FOR THOUGHT

Never make any important decisions while in the shock of bereavement. Do not sell your house, for example, for at least a year. And – alas, I have to say this – resist those dear friends who arrive to pay you sympathy and in the same breath inform you that they were promised certain souvenirs of the departed. Wait a while.

Hugo Vickers
Biographer

THE SHORT VIEW

After my 29-year-old daughter Francesca died of an AIDS-related cancer, only one piece of advice was of any practical use – given by the great Sydney Smith (c. 1830), to a young lady in low spirits. 'Take a short view of life, no further than tea or dinner.'

Elisabeth Luard
Author

171

LIFE AFTER DEATH

As a recently bereaved widow, I have made some rules to keep myself fit (essential now: who will look after me if I am ill?) and to alleviate my sorrow.

1. A proper routine of regular meals. With no one else to cook for, it is all too easy to slip into the habit of snacking on coffee and biscuits.
2. Ask friends in to meals. As well as being a social occasion this makes me cook.
3. Try not to tell people how sad and lonely I feel.
4. Talk to the cat a lot.

And a last thought from observation: don't get married again too soon. I've seen too many newly bereaved marry in haste and bitterly regret it at leisure.

Mrs Gerhard Bulle

WITH US STILL

Our son Jeremy was twenty-two years old when he was a passenger in a fatal car crash. It was a terrible time for us – so sudden, so unexpected. We got through those first dreadful years by always talking about him and laughing about the funny things he did. This way he was still with us. When I was unsure of what to do in any given situation I would ask myself what Jeremy would have expected of me. We have lived our lives to the full, as he did, and as a family we helped each other through it.

Mrs Cherry Slater

AN OBITUARY TO A SAMOYED DOG

Many people at our hospice have found solace in this poem (its origin is unknown and it goes under a number of titles):

Do not stand at my grave and weep,
I am not there, I do not sleep.
I am a thousand winds that blow,
I am the diamond glints on snow,
I am the sunlight on ripened grain,
I am the gentle autumn rain.
When you awake in the morning's hush
I am the uplifting rush
Of quiet birds in circled flight,
I am soft stars that shine at night.
Do not stand at my grave and cry,
I am not there, I did not die.

Julia Lehmann
Katharine House Hospice Bereavement Team

MEMORIES

It is difficult to live with bereavement, but it helps to collect memories of all the happy days spent together. When these are safely stored, all the good that came from the happier times can be remembered, so that the peace carried in your heart is of a full life that accompanied your own for as long as it was able.

George Baker
Actor

LIMITATION

My mother died very suddenly and I found the only way I could limit my grief so that it didn't overwhelm me was to carry on with my work as a physiotherapist as far as possible. I found that visiting my patients and making an effort to appear cheerful was very therapeutic. Then I was able to let myself go at private moments, an essential release.

Jenny Ellison
Physiotherapist

WONDERFUL

'When you cease to wonder, you cease to live' is an adage from my schooldays which has stayed with me, and it proved its value when my beloved husband died. Devastated, I had 'ceased to wonder' except in the literal sense of what on earth I'd do next. Then one day, driving up to Scotland and blubbing all the way, I happened to stop the car and found myself gazing – in wonder – at the glorious indigo hills. That's when I knew I could go on.

Elizabeth Ashley
Actress

PEACE AT LAST

The following few lines from Edmund Spenser's *The Fairie Queen* were given to me by a resident in our Nursing Home Wing:

Sleep after toil, port after stormy seas,
Ease after war, death after life does greatly please.

Dame Cicely Saunders
Chairman, St Christopher's Hospice

THE GOLDEN YEARS

Age is something that doesn't matter,
unless you are a cheese.

BILLIE BURKE

DAY BY DAY

When one is young it is necessary to consider the future and plan ahead. When one is old it is better to take life a day or two at a time and enjoy or suffer the present.

Lady Barbirolli

A FRESH START

When the children leave home you should do so too! Start a new life in a smaller abode and ruthlessly pare down all your possessions. You will find it totally liberating.

Una Stubbs
Actress

GIVE AWAY

When you're getting on a bit, give away a few family treasures at Christmas or birthdays. They are far better used sooner than later.

Lady Georgina Coleridge
Journalist and author

TICK, TICK

I 'tune' my hearing-aid in every morning by listening to the ticking of my alarm clock. When the sound seems about right I leave it on that setting all day and never have to adjust it. I'm not very deaf, but I have been told that it is better to start with the appliance before one needs it desperately so that one can get used to it without too much stress.

Vernon Russell-Smith
Garden designer

HEAR THIS

Do not despise the NHS deaf aid. It has an extra switch for when telephones, concert halls, churches, etc. are wired to be user-friendly. It is conspicuous, so people speak up. Moreover it is free!

The Rt. Hon. James Ramsden

NON-SLIP

On the principle (usually true) that the elderly will get more pleasure from a pampering present than a purely practical one, nice-smelling toiletries are a happy choice. But avoid bath oils. One drop too many can turn a bath tub into a skating rink – an extremely serious hazard for the less agile, especially those who live alone.

Anne Stanley
Retired nurse

SAFETY FIRST

If an elderly person is moving house he or she should always consider installing a shower. Getting in and out of the bath can be a risky business and a shower is much safer to use, especially if it has a built-in seat.

Elizabeth, Viscountess Cowdray

TWO'S COMPANY

To an elderly person living alone, photographs can be very companionable. But if you are going to give one, perhaps of yourself, it will give more pleasure and comfort if it has the recipient in it too.

Mrs Amy Goodchild

KEEPSAKES

After the difficult task of choosing a favourite picture of our two daughters from their last photographic session, we were left with a bundle of extremely good also-rans it seemed a shame not to use. So I picked out twelve, one for each month of the coming new year, and had them made up into calendars for the girls' grandparents. Any good company specializing in personalized stationery will do this, and the recipients swore they were the nicest Christmas presents they had.

Lavinia Dargie
Interior designer

ALL CHANGE

The all-important thing about growing old is never to get stale or set, to adjust to the different periods in your life, and to change with the times you live in.

Katie Boyle
TV personality and agony aunt

THE VOICE OF EXPERIENCE

My husband and I are both ninety years old. We have very different temperaments, so the 'right temperament' can hardly be said to be the secret of longevity. Nevertheless, one's attitude to life probably does count, and part of that attitude must surely be *acceptance*. Old people can't expect to be trouble free but they can feel lucky that they are still able to be plagued by forgetfulness, stiffness and general slowing up.

I always remember a story I heard in the thirties when I was teaching in the Potteries. An old man was leaning on the cemetery wall, coughing his heart out. A passer-by condoled with him in his plight. 'Thanks,' replied the sufferer, 'but there's many a poor soul lying on t'other side of this wall who'd be glad to have my cough.'

The Countess of Longford

TIME WARP

'Time flies when you're having fun' – but as one grows older life isn't necessarily that much fun, though time certainly flies. It's worth reflecting that the one area where the latter is a blessing is in the garden. Whereas waiting for a garden to mature when one was twenty was just too long, when one is older a seedling is a sapling in the twinkling of an eye.

The Lady Wardington

ALLELUIA

Here are some thoughts to put old age into perspective. We senior citizens have survived so many changes – not all of them for worse. We were born before penicillin, polio shots, frozen food, photo-copiers, contact lenses, videos, frisbees and the Pill. We were before radar, credit cards, split atoms, laser beams and ballpoint pens; before dishwashers, tumble-dryers, electric blankets, air conditioners; and before man walked on the moon.

We got married first and lived together after-wards. We thought 'fast food' was what you ate in Lent, a 'Big Mac' was an oversized raincoat and 'crumpet' was what we had for tea. We existed before house husbands, computer dating and dual careers, and 'sheltered accommodation' was where we waited for a bus.

We were before daycare centres, group homes and disposable nappies. We had never heard of FM radio, tape decks, electronic typewriters, artificial hearts, word-processors or young men wearing ear-rings. For us 'time sharing' was togetherness, a 'chip' was a piece of wood or a fried potato, 'hardware' meant nuts and bolts and 'software' just wasn't a word.

Before 1940 'Made in Japan' meant junk, the term 'making out' referred to how you did in your exams, a 'stud' was something that fastened your collar and 'going all the way' meant staying on the double decker to the bus depot. In our day cigarette smoking was fashionable, grass was mown, coke was kept in the coal hole and a joint was served up for lunch on Sunday. A gay person was the life and soul of the party and Aids just meant beauty treat-ment or help for someone in trouble.

We who were born before 1940 must be tough – and by the grace of God we have survived! Alleluia!

Richard Good,
from his seventieth birthday speech

WHAT'S WORSE?

> Growing old is a terrible bore.
> A condition you can't just ignore.
> You can't see to write,
> Your shoes get too tight,
> And your hearing becomes very poor.
>
> Your faculties go in reverse.
> Your health is a drain on your purse.
> But all I can say,
> At the end of the day,
> The alternative's probably worse.

Audrey Wardington

HOW TO TELL WHEN YOU ARE GETTING OLD

Everything hurts, and what doesn't hurt doesn't work.

The gleam in your eyes is from the sun hitting your bifocals.

You feel as if it's the morning after the night before, but you haven't been anywhere.

You get winded playing cards.

Your children begin to look middle-aged.

You know all the answers, but no one asks you the questions.

You need glasses to find your glasses.

You turn out the lights for financial reasons, not romantic ones.

You sit on a rocking chair and can't get it going.

Your knees buckle but your belt won't.

Your house is too big and your medicine cupboard is too small.

And your back goes out more often than you do.

Jenny Candy
Katharine House Hospice Bereavement Team

INDEX OF HINTS

181

INDEX OF CONTRIBUTORS